THE BOTTOMLINE ON ROI

Third Edition

*Benefits and Barriers to Measuring
Learning, Performance Improvement,
and Human Resources Programs*

Patricia Pulliam Phillips, Ph.D.

ROI INSTITUTE®

For additional copies of this publication, contact the HRDQ Customer Service Team at:

Phone: 800-633-4533
             610-279-2002
Fax: 610-279-0524
Online: www.HRDQstore.com

ISBN: 978-1-58854-904-4

Publisher: Martin Delahoussaye
Editorial development: Christina Giampa
Cover design: Carina Ahren
Cover image by Nik Merkulov/Shutterstock.com. Image used under license from
Shutterstock.com. HRDQ and the HRDQ logo are registered trademarks of
Organization Design and Development, Inc. Interior design: Integrative Ink

Printed in the United States of America on recycled paper.

0579E3BK
EN-03-JN-17

TABLE OF CONTENTS

In Memory of

William Kirk Smith, Ph.D.

FOREWORD
A Conversation with Jack

A typical foreword includes the insights and support of someone recognized in the field or specialty about which a book is written. In the second edition of this book, Jack Phillips wrote the foreword. But, in this edition, we, the publishers and author, wanted Jack to address specific questions that may be of interest to readers. This conversation with Jack offers insights, directly from him, into the evolution of the methodology described in this book; the status of its application; and where Jack sees the application of the process going forward.

Ten Questions for Jack Phillips

Patti: Jack, what forces led you to develop this methodology?

Jack: The spark for my very first ROI study was a question from an executive about the value of a program. This was in 1973, when the chief engineer at Lockheed asked me to show the impact and actual monetary contribution of the cooperative education program. At that time, we had 350 co-ops from 16 universities, alternating work and school. The funding for this program was on my budget as the co-op director, and my budget was charged to the chief engineer's budget. This was my first "show me the money" request.

Apart from that spark, there were some other forces. First, I was completing a master's degree in decision sciences (quantitative methods for business), and I wanted to make sure that my methodology was credible, reliable, and valid. At the same time, the study must satisfy an executive's thirst for conservative, easy-to-understand data. With my engineering background, I wanted to know how things worked or not. I had a curiosity to see if this program was adding the value that we thought it was. The executive request, the need for a credible process, and a desire to show the value of what we do were the early forces.

Patti: How has the process evolved since 1973?

Jack: Because it worked so well for me in that first study, I began to fine-tune the process. That first study helped me develop good relationships with my clients, improve support for the co-op program, improve the co-op program, and, yes, continue the funding for the program. With these huge benefits, we had to make the process better and make it user-friendly. I kept working with my own projects at Lockheed, Stockham Valves & Fittings, and Vulcan Materials Company. I had moved from being a member of the learning team to head of learning to head of HR in two consecutive companies at that point. We were fortunate to publish the first book on training evaluation in the USA (*Handbook of Training Evaluation and Measurement Methods,* 1983). It set the tone for evaluation, and in the book, we supported the work of Don Kirkpatrick. Don wrote his first book on training evaluation 11 years later, in 1994. With the publication of our first book, the methodology really caught on globally as well as in the USA, although there were some challenges about pushing analysis all the way to ROI.

Patti: Where are we today in terms of adoption?

Jack: Fast-forward to today, there are over 75 books that support this methodology, published in 38 languages. Over 5,000 organizations are using this methodology, making it the most-used evaluation system in the world. It has been adopted by 26 federal governments and dozens of large non-governmental organizations (NGOs) such as the United Nations. Almost all the Fortune 500 organizations are using it in some function, and almost 100 universities are now using one or more of the books for bachelors, masters, or doctoral students. Standards were developed and approved by users along the way. It is regarded as user-friendly, professor-friendly, and, more importantly, CEO- and top executive-friendly.

Patti: Have we reached the tipping point?

Jack: We have in some countries. In the USA, we have reached the tipping point. In 2015, *Chief Learning Officer* magazine reported that, in a study of 335 chief learning officers (CLOs), 71.2 percent of CLOs are either using ROI or plan to use ROI. That's impressive. *Training* magazine estimates that well over half of their list of "125 Best Organizations" is using the ROI Methodology™. The use is quite high in the USA and in some countries in Europe, South America, the Middle East, and Asia, where we are fully operationalized. With business partners in 66 countries, and the list is growing, we will reach the tipping point globally in the next few years.

Patti: How can ROI help an organization?

Jack: ROI is usually implemented in a particular function, although we have had a few organizations that implement this systematically in all the major functions of human resources (HR), quality, technology, and marketing. It helps an organization clearly understand how to improve projects. Many projects go astray for a variety of reasons, or they are sometimes initiated for the wrong reasons. This process shows where a project fails and how to correct it. In essence, it optimizes the ROI in different projects and programs. This optimization can lead to changes in funding streams in the future.

Patti: Tell us about the most recent applications.

Jack: When we started this process, we were working primarily with business groups, large manufacturing, and service organizations in a particular country. It quickly caught on with governments, and now we spend most of our time with governments, NGOs, nonprofits, educational institutions, foundations, and healthcare firms. We typically move through different applications, with 22 applications, now including a green and sustainability application as well as an application for meetings and events. We are tackling certain industries. For example, *Measuring ROI in Healthcare,* one of our major books, is aimed at bringing this accountability in all phases and functions of healthcare delivery. We are doing the same in governments with publications about the use of ROI in governments. We are also taking the methodology to more countries and cultures to make it adaptable to any type of environment.

Patti: What are the challenges for the use of ROI?

Jack: There are some classic challenges that get in the way. First and foremost is the fear of the results. If a program is not working, no one really wants to see data that exposes the failure. We try to overcome this barrier by emphasizing process improvement as this level of evaluation is pursued. Also, we encourage organizations to be proactive and take steps to show the value before they are being asked to do that. Being requested to show value places you in a defensive mode with a short time frame to deliver results. The outcome, unfortunately, is often disastrous.

The second barrier is the lack of time to do this. With teams already strapped with too many tasks and too many expectations, it is hard to add more evaluation to the process. The key is to start the process early, and not try to measure and evaluate all the way to ROI, but to design for ROI from the very beginning. This approach provides better results and takes fewer resources to actually measure it. Also, we have to face the fact that we have underinvested in measurement, evaluation, and analytics in the learning and HR space. We have to invest more, and we can convince our sponsors to invest more, when we can show the value of what we can do with this type of analysis.

The third barrier is the perceived complexity of this process. This is really a myth—not reality. Logical, practical steps are used, following a classic logic model that has been slightly enhanced to be more credible. Mathematics are kept to a minimum, and software and other tools are available to make it easier. The fact that it is the most-used evaluation system in the world attests to its user-friendly approach. But, until someone understands it and starts using it, they think it's too complex.

The fourth barrier is that they just don't know how to do it. This level of accountability is not built into many of the programs preparing professionals for their chosen field. With no training and little experience, it seems too difficult. We are trying to overcome this by offering our ROI Certification™ in a variety of different formats and delivery methods for individuals. To date, over 12,000 individuals have followed the path of ROI Certification, with about 5,000 now achieving the designation of Certified ROI Professional (CRP). The criteria for completion are of the highest standards, requiring participants to complete an ROI study that meet those standards. Some participants engage in the process merely to acquire the knowledge. Others engage with the intent of completing requirements for certification, but due to job changes and other reasons, they do not.

Patti: In analytics, many of the proponents of predictive analytics usually don't talk about ROI and think it's not connected. What are your thoughts?

Jack: The two go together. In a predictive relationship, we are trying to show how one variable, X, predicts another variable, Y. When this is validated, it becomes an operational tool, often stimulating some interesting reactions from the management team. They often ask, "How much does it costs if we do more X, and what will be the additional value coming out of Y?" This is the ROI question.

Almost all types of analytics lead to ROI. As you often say, "All roads lead to ROI." Each year, we partner with the Center for Talent Reporting and the Institute for Corporate Productivity (i4cp) to produce a human capital analytics practice survey. We are trying to understand how analytics teams are actually functioning. The last study, from over 300 dedicated human capital analytics practices, reveals some interesting data. For the first time, the number-one project undertaken by these teams is measuring the impact and ROI. The number-four project is forecasting ROI. Consequently, ROI is becoming an integrated part of analytics, as it should be. After all, ROI is the ultimate accountability.

Patti: There is much talk about big data. How does ROI work with big data?

Jack: Although there is no clear definition of what is meant by big data, we assume that it's a very large quantity of data that we are analyzing, examining relationships between data. Essentially, we are running all the numbers to see what is connected. We are looking for significant correlations, and if it is significant enough, the causation is assumed. Sometimes, that is a mistake. There is another problem with big data. It often needs scrubbing to make it usable. Sometimes, the efforts to clean it up prohibit use of all the big data.

Consequently, it's helpful to think of small data projects. Projects that need to be evaluated. For example, one of our published case studies is an ROI study on 25 executives involved in a very expensive external coaching program. The ROI analysis shows a high positive ROI for investing in these 25 executives. If these participants are selected in an unbiased way, then these are very good results to begin to make some decisions about the program. This certainly tells us that this program for this group was successful. We can expand that as we need it. This is much better than a big data analysis revealing that there is a significant correlation between coaching expenditures and profits (with no causation).

We don't necessarily need big data analysis for ROI inside an organization. Many projects or programs are implemented with a small pilot group to see if it's working. After all, if it does not work, we don't want to expose the program or solution to the entire organization. Program trials are not big data by their purpose and scope, but they can certainly be very meaningful and often lead to some very important decision-making opportunities.

Patti: What's the future of ROI?

Jack: We will continue to expand the use of ROI into other applications, such as innovation, social media, risk management, and culture. We will move into more segments involving the social sector with books and applications for universities, nonprofits, religious groups, and foundations. We will also push this into other countries, with hopes of having 100 countries actively involved in the next five to ten years. We will continue to push publications by contributing approximately five books a year to support these efforts.

From all indications, the use of ROI as a tool to evaluate and improve noncapital investments is here to stay and will be a part of the future of all organizations. We will help ensure this by incorporating a book into a course in the finance and accounting field, *Measuring the Return on Noncapital Investments,* to complement what is typically achieved now for the capital expenditures.

In summary, the future is bright. ROI will always be needed for important projects. All roads lead to ROI.

Jack J. Phillips, Ph.D.
Developer of the ROI Methodology™
Chairman and Co-Founder, ROI Institute, Inc.

INTRODUCTION

Consider this scenario: Sydney Mitchell has been serving as CEO for Global Communications for the past nine months. She has a reputation for being aggressive in meeting goals, yet she is pragmatic and fair. In her previous organization, Sydney increased profits as well as customer satisfaction ratings while reducing staff and positioning the company as one of the 100 Best Companies to Work For®. Before making significant changes in Global Communications' organizational structure, Sydney is giving each function one year to make strides toward meeting strategic objectives. These strategic objectives focus on increasing profits, market share, customer satisfaction ratings, and employee satisfaction ratings. Sydney communicates these objectives very clearly during her monthly learning sessions with employees, team leaders, and executives to help them understand the meaning and importance of each objective.

With three months remaining in the year, Sydney is in another round of meetings with the executives of each function to get status reports. She has been relatively pleased with the results in the marketing, human resources (HR), and distribution functions. Today she is meeting with the President of GlobalCom University, Global Communications' corporate university.

Donald Hodges is the President of GlobalCom University. He was handpicked by the past CEO and believes that the university is making a difference. He always receives rave reviews from participants after each program. Donald is ready for Sydney. He has a flashy slide presentation that includes all of his program evaluations.

Sydney enters the room.

Sydney: Hi, Donald. It's nice to see you. The place looks great, and everyone seems really busy.

Donald: Yes, Sydney. We're developing 12 new programs.

Sydney: Really? What are these programs?

Donald: Well, we're developing a new communications program as well as revising our orientation program to include our new benefits package. We've also had requests from employees to offer programs they're interested in, including a dress-for-success program, a time management program, and a business etiquette program. And we're developing a leadership program similar to one that I attended recently and really enjoyed. I think the managers will enjoy it as well.

Sydney: Hmmmmm. How much time does it take to develop these programs?

Donald: Oh, not long; about a week for each day of training at the most. We have our four program developers working on three programs each. I estimate it will take a few months to develop all 12 programs.

Sydney: I see. A few months…

Donald: Come on into the conference room, Sydney. I want to share our accomplishments thus far!

Sydney: Great, I'd really like to see.

Donald boots up the presentation. He goes through all the preliminary issues, and then he gets to the results of the past nine months.

Donald: In the past nine months, we have developed 10 new programs, offered 1,724 hours of training, had 3,680 employees attend training, and received an average of 4.5 out of 5 on the program satisfaction rating. So, basically, we have developed new training, we offered some of the new programs as well as some of the old favorites, and the employees attending training seem to think we're moving in the right direction.

Sydney: Thanks for the update, Donald. Do we know about the success of these programs on the job?

Donald: No, not specifically, but we are confident that they are adding value.

Sydney: How do you know you're adding value?

Donald: Because of the feedback we receive.

Sydney: What kind of feedback do you receive?

Donald: Many of the participants tell us that they have been very successful with what they have learned.

Sydney: So, you've actually had a follow-up after each program?

Donald: No, not exactly. We just receive random comments.

Sydney: So you have no organized way of knowing about the success of your programs?

Donald: Well, it's not a formal follow-up, but we still receive good feedback.

Sydney: I see. Well, thanks, Donald. I'd like to meet with you next Monday to discuss the contribution GlobalCom University is making to the organization.

Put yourself in Donald's position. How do you think the meeting went? Now, put yourself in Sydney's position. Did Donald demonstrate value for the corporate university? Did he show how programs connect with profit or market share? Did he make connections with measures of customer satisfaction or employee satisfaction? What will be the fate of GlobalCom University?

All too often, this same scenario plays out in organization after organization. Program and project owners are excited about the activity around what they do, and it is this activity that often provides the basis for decisions about programs—decisions that often result in smaller budgets, fewer staff, less status, more skepticism, and growing frustration for everyone. Activity does not translate to results. Activity, while necessary to get the job done, represents costs. Costs get cut. Results, however, reflect the benefits of an investment. Investments are allocated. Learning and development, performance improvement, HR, and other functions that support the business within an organization are shifting from an activity-based paradigm to a results-based paradigm.

From Activity to Results

For decades, activity-based organizations implemented programs without a clearly defined business need or an assessment of the performance issues driving a business need. Senior leaders accepted many functions, such as learning and development and HR, as necessary costs to ensure that the human side of the organization remained intact and well trained. Billions of dollars were spent on developing people, but few questions were asked. Activity-focused organizations failed to set specific measurable objectives to position programs for results. In addition, they failed to prepare participants to achieve results. They did not make an effort to prepare the work environment to support the transfer of knowledge, skill, and information to actual performance. Programs moved forward without plans to ensure that success would occur after the content was disseminated. Organizations that focused solely on activity made little, if any, effort to build partnerships with key managers, and they neglected to measure results in terms that resonated with key managers and executives, including the cost-benefit comparison. Activity-focused organizations placed emphasis on input rather than outcomes. But, today, things have changed.

Today, senior leaders are asking questions. They want to know what value investing in initiatives brings to the organization. They want to know the business impact of programs and projects as well as the ROI. Many organizations are heeding these demands by focusing their efforts on results.

Results-based organizations ensure that programs link to specific business measures and that the assessment of performance effectiveness occurs so that the right performance is addressed given the business needs. Specific, measurable objectives for behavior change and business impact are developed routinely. These objectives are communicated to participants to prepare them to achieve results and to position the programs for success. In addition, results-based organizations prepare the environment for knowledge transfer by developing transfer strategies, describing who needs to do what and when they need to do it in order to put knowledge, skill, and information acquisition to use. Partnerships with key managers and clients exist in results-based organizations, and measures are taken to ensure that programs and projects are achieving the results important to these partners. Finally, results-based organizations plan for and report outputs and outcomes and answer the basic question: "So what?"

Many of these results-based organizations have adopted the ROI Methodology described in this book. While the adoption of such a process does not cause an immediate shift from one extreme of the activity-results continuum to the other, methodical, systematic implementation does enable an organization to move toward a results-based paradigm. Over the past few decades, the ROI process has been vastly successful in helping leaders and professionals address their accountability needs, describe program results in terms that resonate with all stakeholders, and provide data useful in making improvements to all types of programs. Thousands of individuals have been trained in the process, and hundreds of organizations in 66 countries, to date, are applying it. So, why does it work for so many organizations?

Why the ROI Methodology Works

The ROI Methodology presents a balanced set of measures. ROI is the ultimate measure of success, given that it requires that both program benefits and costs be converted to money so that a direct comparison can be made; however, it is not the only measure of success. Additional measures provide a more complete story of program success and help to explain how the ROI is developed. In order to develop this balanced set of measures, a process must be put in place. The ROI Methodology provides this process. Step by step, program owners and evaluators can conduct comprehensive ROI studies while ensuring consistency in their approach. Through the use of standards, or guiding principles, the process can be replicated time and time again.

The ROI Methodology balances research and statistical methods with practical application. Fundamental research principles are always followed, but programs and processes are not researched without end. Organizations need data, and they need it quickly, so a balance is established between how much to invest in an evaluation and the value of the data evolving from it.

A process must be scalable, meaning that, if it works for one function, it should work for another of greater or lesser scale. The ROI Methodology is scalable. Organizations applying it in learning, HR, and performance improvement often expand its use to other functions, such as marketing, meetings and events, and quality. This scalability allows programs of all types to be evaluated using the same process, thereby developing results that can actually be compared between programs.

Perhaps the most important aspect of the ROI Methodology is that it is credible to senior managers. The ROI metric is familiar to accountants and financiers in all organizations. It is fundamental. In addition, senior leaders can easily see how the connection transpires between a program and its results. They also appreciate the conservative approach required by the ROI Methodology, which guarantees that the ROI is understated rather than inflated.

So, what is ROI? The answer lies in Chapter 1.

About This Book

The first edition of *The Bottomline on ROI* was awarded the 2003 International Society for Performance Improvement (ISPI) Award of Excellence for Outstanding Instructional Communication. The book reviews were good, and many people wrote or commented that the book provided a good overview of a complex topic. This feedback provided an indication that the book achieved its objective: to provide a simple overview of the ROI Methodology to help readers decide whether or not they want to pursue the process further.

The second edition, published in 2012, added new content, including information clarifying key issues that surround the topic of ROI. Additionally, it incorporated new research and an entire section responding to frequently asked questions. Nevertheless, it did not lose its focus—offering a simple overview of what is now the most applied approach to measuring learning, HR, and performance improvement programs. In developing the second edition of the book, ROI Institute® partnered with HRDQ to develop a Participant Guide and Facilitator Guide to support organizations as they build fundamental skills in the ROI Methodology. This one-day workshop, *The Bottomline on ROI*, has proven to be an important way in which organizations introduce ROI to their teams. Additionally, ROI Institute and HRDQ have partnered to offer a virtual boot camp, a one-week fast-paced introduction to the ROI Methodology.

The topic of ROI continues to appear in books, on conference agendas, and in trade publications. Our applications of the process continue to expand. Our work with environmental, health, and safety initiatives has grown, as has our work with NGOs and faith-based organizations, not to mention the expansion of our global reach with private sector and government organizations. The processes to which the ROI Methodology are applied are endless, but it is the learning and development, performance improvement, and HR areas where we find our grounding and where we invest much of our energy, as in the case of this new edition.

The Bottomline on ROI presents the rationale for developing and implementing a comprehensive measurement and evaluation process that includes ROI. The book presents and explores an evaluation process that is credible to key stakeholders. Implementing the ROI Methodology generates a set of balanced measures, including participant reaction, satisfaction, and planned action; learning; application; impact; ROI; and intangible benefits. This scorecard provides a clear indication of the actual impact of programs, processes, and initiatives.

This third edition of the book remains a simple overview of the ROI Methodology, yet it also updates readers on how organizations are applying the process. In this third edition, readers will learn:

- Why ROI is as relevant today as it has been in the past.

- New applications of the ROI Methodology.

- How to forecast ROI at different levels, using simple techniques (a new chapter).

- How to report the success of programs and projects in ways that resonate with senior executives.

- How to choose technologies that support the ROI Methodology.

Included in this edition is a case study describing the application of the process. Additionally, readers will find a scenario describing a presentation of results to a senior leadership team.

Readers will not find detailed steps and calculations in this book. However, they will find enough information to acquire a basic understanding of the ROI Methodology. This book can be used for the following purposes:

- Learning the basics of ROI

- Providing an overview of ROI to team members

- Teaching team members the fundamentals of ROI

- Persuading managers that ROI is the right choice for an organization

- Beginning to develop a measurement and evaluation strategy

Whether readers are seeking an initial understanding of ROI evaluation or looking for ways to generate support for ROI within an organization, this book provides a fundamental understanding of ROI and how it can be implemented. In addition to new content, this book includes the following:

- Key issues driving the need to measure programs and projects

- Benefits of developing ROI

- Profile of typical organizations that are using ROI

- Symptoms indicating that an organization is ready for ROI

- Pieces of the evaluation puzzle necessary to build a comprehensive measurement and evaluation system

- Criteria for effective ROI implementation

- The ROI Methodology™ model that will produce a balanced set of measures

- A communication process model for ensuring effective communication both during and after the process

- Steps to begin to implement the ROI Methodology

After reading the book, you may want answers to additional questions about ROI and how it will serve your needs. You can find these answers through various workshops and resources described in the back of the book. If, after reading the book, you are interested in sharing the process with your team, you should purchase the entire tool kit for every member. We at ROI Institute in partnership with HRDQ have created a Participant Workbook so that organizations can build capacity in the basics of ROI on their own. We have also developed a Facilitator Guide to help you to teach the process to your team. Details on this opportunity are provided in the back of the book.

Acknowledgments

No project is the work of just one individual. First, thanks go to CEP Press for publishing the first edition of the book and to HRDQ for taking on the second and now third editions and developing the tool kit. Since HRDQ adopted this book, we have had great success introducing the ROI Methodology to new users as well as those who support the process within organizations.

Many thanks go specifically to Martin Delahoussaye, Vice President of Publishing at HRDQ, for his continued support in our work, and to Christina Giampa, Development Editor at HRDQ, for improving the manuscript to make this book better than what we would have developed alone. We know that by collaborating with HRDQ on this book, we are helping organizations to gain a better understanding of what ROI is, what it is not, and how the ROI Methodology can position their programs for success.

As with all of our projects, special thanks go to the team at ROI Institute. Particular thanks go to Hope Nicholas, our Director of Publications. Hope makes our publishing work happen, in spite of our efforts to make it difficult for her. Thanks also go to Anita and Crystal for all they do to support Jack and me as we travel the world helping clients move forward with their measurement and evaluation practice.

Finally, thanks go to Jack for the work he has done and for the way in which he allows others to take his work and run with it. Your passion for your work and your need to continue striving for perfection are inspiring. You have taught me how to balance the serious with the not so serious and how to tackle a project with laser focus. Your greatest gift, however, is in making me laugh—no one does it better. Thank you for being my biggest fan and for supporting me in all my efforts.

CHAPTER 1: ROI DEFINED

ROI continues to be a hot topic in the learning and development, HR, and performance improvement circles. In fact, never before has it had the attention that it does today. *Chief Learning Officer* Business Intelligence Board's 2016 Measurement and Metrics study indicates that 70 percent of CLOs report that they are either using or plan to use ROI as a demonstration of learning's contribution to the organization. The 2016 study from ROI Institute, i4cp, and Center for Talent Reporting, *The Promising State of Human Capital Analytics*, reports that measuring impact and ROI is the most pursued type of human capital analytics project.

While some might argue that measuring the ROI of their programs is a luxury, not a necessity, we beg to differ. Without measurement, evaluation, and ROI, how can an organization know why they are implementing programs, how to position programs for success, and what results come from those programs? They can't. However, the question remains for many professionals facing this challenge—what, exactly, is ROI?

The ROI Calculation

ROI is a financial metric describing the return on investment in a program, process, or initiative. It compares the monetary benefits of an investment to the investment itself. ROI is considered the ultimate measure of program success for a variety of reasons, one of which is that it requires normalizing program benefits and costs through the use of money so that the two can be compared mathematically. In this one metric, economic contribution is apparent. The concept of ROI has been used for centuries (Sibbett 1997). This single statistic can be compared to other opportunities inside or outside the company. There are many metrics that compare the financial benefits of an investment to the cost. Those most often used for programs such as learning and development, performance improvement, and HR are the benefit-cost ratio (BCR) and the ROI percentage. Occasionally, a payback period (PP) is calculated to determine at what point in time a program will break even. Net present value (NPV) is used to forecast return on investment for large purchases such as equipment and software. Following are brief descriptions of each.

Benefit-Cost Ratio (BCR)

The BCR is one of the oldest measures of return on investment. An output of cost-benefit analysis (CBA), the BCR compares the monetary benefits of an investment to the cost, resulting in a ratio. Grounded in welfare economics and public finance, CBA has historically served as a feasibility tool to justify government involvement in the economy and to examine the extent of government's influence on the private sector and on the welfare of society at large (Thompson 1980; Kearsley 1982; Nas 1996; Phillips 1997b).

The following is the BCR in formula form:

$$BCR = \frac{\textbf{Benefits}}{\textbf{Costs}}$$

The following steps lead to the BCR:

- Identify the annual benefits or gains from implementing a program.

- Convert benefits to monetary value using profit, cost savings, or cost avoidance associated with the investment.

- Determine the cost (or investment) of the program.

- Identify the intangible benefits of program implementation.

- Compare the monetary benefits to the program costs.

- Compare the result to some alternative program or a standard for acceptance.

Reported as a ratio, the BCR describes how the annual monetary benefits returned compare to the cost. For example, if a program returns $650,000 in monetary benefits from profit, cost savings, and/or cost avoidance over a one-year period and costs the organization $350,000, the BCR, which represents break-even, is this:

$$BCR = \frac{\$650,000}{\$350,000} = 1.86:1$$

This BCR indicates that for every $1 invested in the program, $1.86 is returned. The classic decision-making criterion for the BCR is that anything over a 1:1 BCR, which represents break-even, is acceptable.

Return on Investment (ROI)

ROI is the ultimate measure of the profitability of an investment and is the classic tool used to report this profitability. Applied for centuries by financiers, the metric became widespread in the 1960s for measuring operating performance in industry (Horngren 1982). Today, this simple metric is standard in business and is now used in non-business settings when reporting the economic contribution of all types of investments.

BCR was historically used as a feasibility tool in deciding whether to move forward on projects. ROI was a measure of past performance, basing assumptions on historical data. Today, ROI is commonly developed up front to forecast benefits and is used to make investment decisions, whereas BCR is now commonly used as a post-investment measure of actual results. ROI compares annual earnings (or net program benefits) to the investment (or program costs). Unlike its cousin, BCR, ROI is reported as a percentage and represents the annual net benefits returned beyond the initial investment. The steps used to develop the data necessary to calculate the ROI are similar to those used to calculate the BCR; however, the difference is in the formula, as shown in the following equation:

$$\text{ROI} = \frac{\text{Net Benefits}}{\text{Costs}} \times 100$$

Using the earlier example, for a program achieving $650,000 in monetary benefits and requiring an investment of $350,000, the ROI is this:

$$\text{ROI} = \frac{\$650,000 - \$350,000}{\$350,000} \times 100 = 86\%$$

The resulting ROI indicates that, for every $1 invested in the program, that dollar is returned, plus there is a gain of 86 cents ($0.86). The 86 cents represents an 86% *return* on the investment. While this seems like a reasonable return, acceptance of an 86% ROI is dependent on the standard to which this ROI is compared.

What makes a good ROI?

An ROI is only as good as that to which it is compared. Use the following guidelines to help you establish your target ROI:
- Set the ROI at the same level as other investments (e.g., 18%).
- Set the ROI slightly higher than the level of other investments (e.g., 25%).
- Set the ROI at break-even (e.g., 0%).
- Ask the client to help set the target ROI.

Payback Period (PP)

Periodically, it may be useful to estimate the time at which the organization can expect to recoup its investment in a program. This PP is calculated by comparing the initial investment with the annual cash flows or monetary benefits due to the program. The equation is simply a reverse of the BCR.

PP is reported in terms of a number of months or years. Using the earlier example, the PP for a program reaping $650,000 in monetary benefits and costing the organization $350,000 is this:

$$PP = \frac{\$350,000}{\$650,000} = .54$$

The output of multiplying .54 by 12 months indicates a PP for this program of 6.48 months. This tells decision makers that they can expect to recover their investment in less than one year. This PP is compared to that of other potential investments or to a predetermined standard. ROI, BCR, and PP are appropriate when comparing the monetary benefits of investing in programs that support the development, recruitment, management, engagement, and process improvement of HR. While people are assets to an organization, they are not treated the same way in the accounting books as other assets, such as equipment, land, and buildings. In addition, many people-focused initiatives are short-term in nature, meaning that they take only a few months, weeks, or even days to fully implement. Bearing this in mind, it is important to remember that a payoff within the first year of such an investment is desirable, if not required (Phillips and Phillips 2007).

Net Present Value (NPV)

Because the issue of NPV is important to the ROI discussion, it is worth a mention here. NPV is one of several discounted cash flow (DCF) methods that account for the time value of money and that are used for long-range decision making.

Using NPV, expected cash inflows (program benefits) and outflows (program costs) are discounted to the present value at a given point in time, using a preselected discount rate. The assumed benefits over a period of time (discounted at the determined discount rate) are totaled, and the initial investment is subtracted. The future benefits and costs are reduced to a single present dollar value. If the present value of benefits is greater than the investment, the program is assumed to be a good investment (Nas 1996; Friedlob and Plewa 1996).

DCF methods are useful if someone is investing in technology, has large capital expenses for which a constant stream of benefits is ensured, or is investing today for some future realized return. For noncapital expenditures or programs that are considered short-term and from which benefits are expected in the near term, however, DCF methods are not appropriate.

Other Measures of Financial Return

ROI is the topic of many a conversation. It is good news that the overall discussion is taking place, particularly in areas where ROI has not historically been a consideration. The bad news, however, is that these conversations sometimes lead to the creation of creative, albeit meaningless, spins on various financial acronyms. Take ROE, for example, which is defined as "return on equity" from a business perspective. Return on equity is determined by comparing net income to shareholders' equity. ROE is useful for comparing the profitability of a given company to that of other firms in the same industry. It is not a measure suitable for valuing investment in people, processes, and projects. Unfortunately, too many learning and performance improvement professionals define ROE as "return on expectations." While the acronym is clever, it is meaningless in terms of measures of economic contribution. It is important that professionals at all levels and in all functions of an organization at least recognize the difference between what is merely clever and what is meaningful from a business perspective. Table 1 presents a brief list of acronyms representing key financial measures and their associated definitions.

Table 1. Financial Measures

Acronym	Definition	Description
ROI	Return on Investment	Used to evaluate the efficiency or profitability of an investment or to compare the efficiency of a number of investments.
		Calculation: Compares the annual net benefits of an investment to the cost of the investment, expressed as a percentage.
		ROI = (Net Benefits / Costs) × 100
ROE	Return on Equity	Measures a corporation's profitability by revealing how much profit a company generates with the money that shareholders have invested. Used for comparing the profitability of a company to that of other firms in the same industry.
		Calculation: Compares the annual net income to shareholder equity.
		ROE = Net Income / Shareholder Equity
ROA	Return on Assets	Indicates how profitable a company is in relation to its total assets. Measures how efficient management is at using its assets to generate earnings.
		Calculation: Compares annual net income (annual earnings) to total assets, expressed as a percentage.
		ROA = Net Income / Total Assets
ROAE	Return on Average Equity	Modified version of ROA, referring to a company's performance over a fiscal year.
		Calculation: Same as ROA, except the denominator is changed from total assets to average shareholders' equity, which is computed as the sum of the equity value at the beginning and end of the year divided by two.
		ROAE = Net Income / Average Shareholder Equity
ROCE	Return on Capital Employed	Indicates the efficiency and profitability of a company's capital investments. ROCE should always be higher than the rate at which the company borrows; otherwise, any increase in borrowing will reduce shareholders' earnings.
		Calculation: Compares earnings before interest and tax (EBIT) to total assets – current liabilities.
		ROCE = EBIT / Total Assets – Current Liabilities

Acronym	Definition	Description
PV	Present Value	Current worth of a future sum of money or stream of cash flows (C) given a specified rate of return. Important in financial calculations, including NPV, bond yields, and pension obligations.
		Calculation: Divides amount of cash flows (or sum of money) by the interest rate over a period of time.
		$PV = C/(1+r)^t$
NPV	Net Present Value	Measures the difference between the present value of cash inflows and the present value of cash outflows. Another way to put it: measures the present value of future benefits with the present value of the investment.
		Calculation: Compares the value of a dollar today to the value of that same dollar in the future, taking into account a specified interest rate over a specified period of time.
		$NPV = \sum_{t-1}^{T} (C_t/(1+r)^t) - C_0$
IRR	Internal Rate of Return	Makes the NPV of all cash flows from a particular project equal to zero. Used in capital budgeting. The higher the IRR, the more desirable it is to undertake the process.
		Calculation: Follows the NPV calculation as a function of the rate of return. A rate of return for which this function is zero is the internal rate of return.
		$NPV = \sum_{n=0}^{N} (C_n/(1+r)^n) = 0$
PP	Payback Period	Measures the length of time to recover an investment.
		Calculation: Compares the cost of a project to the annual benefits or annual cash inflows.
		$PP = Costs/Benefits$
BCR	Benefit-Cost Ratio	Used to evaluate potential costs and benefits of a project that may be generated if the project is completed. Used to determine financial feasibility.
		Calculation: Compares project annual benefits to its cost.
		$BCR = Benefits/Costs$

Imperfection of Financial Measures

Regardless of the ROI metric used, the calculation alone is an imperfect measurement that must be used in conjunction with other performance measures as part of a measurement and evaluation process (Horngren 1982). Reporting a single financial metric provides evidence of success in terms of what that measure means, but that single measure doesn't tell the whole story. For example, a learning and development function evaluates a performance management program for new store managers. The ROI is 75%. Senior managers ask these questions:

- Is that good? How do you know?

- How did you arrive at 75% ROI?

- Who was involved in the program?

- What prevented you from getting a higher return?

- Can you improve it?

- How do you know that the ROI is due to your program and not the new technology employed in the stores?

Without additional data coupled with a robust methodology, the story is limited to economics only. Other measures of success tell the rest of the ROI story. These measures include the following:

- Input into the process, including target audience, number of people, and cost per person. These measures represent the scope of the program; in other words, this is the investment.

- Participants' reaction to the program, particularly their perception of the relevance of the program's content, the importance the content will have to their jobs, and their intent to apply what they learned in the program. These measures of utility can often provide predictive information regarding the learning and application of the skills (Alliger and Tannenbaum 1997; Warr, Allan, and Birdi 1999; APQC 2000).

- The extent to which learning can be applied immediately following the program so that the application of the new knowledge, skills, and information becomes routine.

- The extent to which new knowledge, skills, and information are applied in order to improve key business measures. In addition, data are collected that describe how the organization's system supports learning transfer and what barriers might prohibit participants from applying what they learn.

- The improvement in business measures as a result of the application of new knowledge, skills, and information learned in the program. Further, these data describe how the improvement is connected to the program versus other influencing factors.

These data explain how the ROI is derived and provide information necessary to improve the program and the system that supports learning transfer. They represent the chain of impact that occurs as organizations invest in their people, projects, and programs.

Rationale for Implementing ROI

Programs, processes, and projects are implemented routinely throughout all types of organizations, but as the costs of these programs escalate, the budgets for these initiatives become targets for others who would like to divert the money to their own projects. The learning and development industry spends billions of dollars annually. The 2016 *State of the Industry Report* from the Association for Talent Development (ATD, formerly ASTD) indicates growth in learning expenditures. As reported in 2015, the industry saw a 1.9 percent increase over 2014 in average spend per employee. In real dollars, the investment went from $1,229 to $1,252 per employee. Additionally, organizations saw an increase in the number of learning hours used per employee, from 32.4 hours in 2014 to 33.5 hours in 2015. While this increase represents continued commitment to learning and development, it also suggests continued expectation for results (ATD, 2016).

Consequences of Ineffective Programs

Ineffective programs bring additional scrutiny and skepticism to bear on all functions within the organization. Many programs do not live up to their promises or expectations. They do not deliver the expected results— at least, not in terms the client understands. When results are insufficient, concern often surrounds the credibility of the evaluation process, the program, and the overall function. As a result, greater constraints and demands are placed on the function. In many cases, the consequences of ineffective practices lead to restructuring, elimination of processes, and sometimes the displacement of staff members. By implementing a sound ROI methodology, organizations can weed out ineffective programs or make existing programs more effective.

Linking to Strategic Initiatives

The need to link processes to the strategic direction of the company applies to all functions—including those focused on employee development and performance. The importance of linking programs to organizational strategy is another major reason to pursue a comprehensive measurement and evaluation process. Management often scrutinizes programs to determine what value they bring to the overall strategy. How do they fit? How will they help the organization to achieve its goal? Are the right programs being offered, and, if so, how do we know? The need to link programs to the organization's strategic objectives and report results that reflect these objectives brings a greater interest in the accountability of such programs and drives the need for ROI.

At-Risk Funding

Departmental resources are at risk when performance is unclear or less than expected. This expectation is often measured by the monetary contributions of its programs and projects. For example, annual budgets are placed at risk by basing them on a threshold ROI. If the minimum ROI is met for key programs, the budget remains level. Exceeding the threshold results in increased budget; falling below the threshold causes a budget reduction. This pay-for-performance process requires the use of an ROI methodology that ensures credible, reliable results.

Top Executive Requirements

Increased interest in ROI from the executive suite is commonplace in many organizations in the United States as well as other countries around the world. Top executives watch their budgets constantly increase. If these various investments are not yielding meaningful results, frustration sets in, and the call for results, including ROI, grows louder. Executives must make appropriate funding decisions based on the impact that programs have on the financial health of their organizations. Without a measure that can be compared across all programs and processes, perception and political interest are the decision levers. While perception and politics may play into decision making, omitting meaningful outcome data places managers and staff who own the programs in an acquiescing, rather than influencing, role. For operational excellence to occur in organizations, programs must drive greater benefits than they cost. ROI is a single metric that can demonstrate those results in terms that executives understand and appreciate.

The Need for Balanced Measures

There is continuous debate as to how much focus to place on ROI versus other measures. Some people prefer soft measures obtained directly from clients and consumers, such as measures of work habits, work climate, and attitudes. Others prefer hard data focused on measures of output, quality, cost, and time. The best approach employs a balanced set of measures that takes into consideration participant preferences, learning, application, change in business measures, the actual ROI, and intangible measures. Data should be examined from a variety of sources, at different time periods, and for different purposes. The need for balanced measures is a major driver of the ROI Methodology, in that it provides financial impact (ROI) along with the other important data.

Desire to Contribute

Individuals engaged in professional work want to know that their efforts make a difference. They need to see that they are making a contribution in terms that managers and executives respect and appreciate. One of the most satisfying elements of program ownership may be showing the ROI of key programs. A comprehensive measurement and evaluation process not only shows the success of a program in terms of schedule, budget, and client feedback but also reflects the actual monetary value added. An impressive ROI provides the final touch to a major program. This type of evaluation serves as evidence for staff, managers, and executives that programs of all types do make a difference.

Benefits of the ROI Methodology

Routine use of the ROI Methodology reaps several benefits. Collectively, these benefits add enough value to develop a positive ROI on implementing the ROI Methodology.

Show the Contribution of Selected Programs

With ROI, both the client and the staff will know the specific contribution of a program. The ROI calculation will show the actual net benefits versus the cost, elevating the evaluation data to a clear level of accountability. This process presents indisputable evidence of program success. When a program succeeds, in many cases, the same type of program can be applied to other areas in the organization. If one division has success with a program, and another division has the same needs, the program should add comparable value to that division, enhancing the overall success of all programs.

Earn the Respect of Senior Management

Demonstrating the impact of programs is one of the most convincing ways to earn the respect and support of the senior management team—and not just for one particular program. Managers respect processes and programs that add bottomline value in terms they understand. ROI evaluation is comprehensive; when applied consistently to several programs, it can convince management that all functions are important investments and not just a source of costs. Mid-level managers will view programs and projects as making a viable contribution to their immediate objectives. ROI is a critical step toward helping leaders and staff to build successful partnerships with the senior management team.

Gain the Confidence of Clients

Evaluation using the ROI Methodology provides clients—those requesting and authorizing programs—a complete set of data to show the overall success of a program. The balanced profile of results from the ROI Methodology provides coverage from different sources, at different time frames, and with both qualitative and quantitative data. Implementing the ROI Methodology provides the information needed to validate the initial decision to move forward with a new program, continue an existing program, or eliminate an ineffective program.

Improve Processes

Because the evaluation process requires that data be collected at multiple time frames, program owners can garner enough information to make adjustments during and after program implementation. These data are helpful in improving future programs by describing which processes are nonproductive and which add value. Thus, ROI evaluation becomes an important process-improvement tool.

Develop a Results-Based Approach

ROI evaluation requires involvement from all stakeholders, including program designers and developers, facilitators, and evaluators. Throughout program design and implementation, the entire team of stakeholders focuses on results. From detailed planning to the actual communication of results, every team member has a responsibility to achieve success. This focus often enhances the evaluation results, because the ultimate outcomes are clearly in mind. In essence, the program begins with the end in mind. Program processes, activities, and steps focus on evaluation measures, from how well participants respond to the program to the actual ROI. As the function demonstrates success, confidence grows, enhancing the results of future program evaluations.

Alter or Eliminate Ineffective Programs

If a program is not going well, and the expected results are not materializing, data from ROI will prompt changes or modifications to the program. These changes can take place during program implementation, so that the final results are positive, or in between program offerings based on the results of comprehensive evaluation. When an organization stays on track with the evaluation process, programs can evolve continuously so as to enhance overall results. On the other hand, a comprehensive ROI evaluation can provide evidence that the program will not achieve desired results. While it takes courage to eliminate a program, this action will reap important benefits in the long term.

ROI on the ROI

Most organizations spend less than 1 percent of their direct budgets on measurement and evaluation processes. This figure considers only the post-program analysis or comprehensive review process. Interjecting accountability throughout a program requires expenditures closer to 3–5 percent of the total budget, a small price to pay given that the payoff includes:

- Preventing the implementation of unnecessary programs (after an evaluation of the pilot program indicates that it will not add value)

- Altering or redesigning existing programs to make them more effective (and less expensive)

- Eliminating unproductive and ineffective programs (thus eliminating their costs)
- Expanding the implementation of successful programs (adding value to other divisions, regions, etc.)

Many organizations keep a running total of the monetary benefits derived from implementing an ROI methodology. In comparing these benefits to the cost of implementation, the results yield a positive "ROI on the ROI."

Candidates for ROI

Accountability does not apply to any one particular type of organization. Bringing accountability to programs and processes is a basic concern for organizations, regardless of their products, services, mission, or scope. Accountability issues exist in organizations during favorable as well as unfavorable economic times. In good economic times, expenditures increase and organizational leaders strive to properly allocate resources. In tough economic times, programs and processes that yield the best results are the most likely to survive reorganization and restructuring efforts. Whether the organization is a large insurance company, a computer manufacturer, a federal or local government agency, or an NGO, a comprehensive evaluation process can help pinpoint the areas in which to invest.

Characteristics of Organizations Using ROI

While the ROI Methodology is suitable for any organization, the organizations currently implementing ROI as part of their evaluation process share some characteristics, such as the following:

Size of the organization. Currently, organizations implementing ROI are generally large. Whether in the public or private sector, large organizations tend to deliver a variety of programs to a diverse target audience—usually throughout a vast geographical area. Organizations delivering a variety of programs usually have some programs they could do without, and it is important to ensure that they are offering the right programs, for the right reasons, at the right times, to the right people. Large organizations also have the budgets necessary to develop comprehensive evaluation approaches. However, ROI should be built into the accountability process in smaller organizations as well. Small organizations have even greater reason to conserve resources and ensure that they are getting the most out of their dollars. Using several cost-saving approaches described later, small organizations (and larger organizations with limited budgets) can implement ROI with credible results.

Size and visibility of the budget. Organizations implementing ROI usually allocate large budgets to programs such as those in the learning, performance improvement, and HR functions. Some organizations allocate as much as $1 billion to these types of programs. The size of the budget holds the attention of the senior management team. Regardless of how it is measured (whether as total budget, expenditure per employee, percentage of payroll, or percentage of revenue), a large budget brings focus to additional measurement and evaluation. Executives demand increased accountability for large expenditures.

Focus on measurement. Typically, organizations implementing ROI focus on establishing a variety of measures throughout the organization. Organizations already using well-known processes such as the Balanced Scorecard and Six Sigma are ideal candidates for the ROI Methodology, because these organizations represent measurement-focused environments.

Key drivers requiring additional accountability. The presence of the drivers discussed earlier brings additional focus to accountability. Drivers for accountability include ineffective programs, at-risk funding, and top requirements, among other issues. These drivers create the need to change current practices. In most situations, multiple drivers create interest in ROI accountability

Level of change taking place. Organizations using ROI are usually undergoing significant change. As an organization adjusts to competitive pressures, it is transforming, restructuring, and reorganizing. Significant change often increases interest in bottomline issues, resulting in a need for greater accountability.

Symptoms That an Organization Is Ready for ROI

Several revealing symptoms indicate that an organization is ready to implement ROI. Many of these symptoms reflect the key drivers discussed earlier, which cause pressure to pursue ROI. Some of the most obvious signs that an organization is ready for ROI include the following:

Pressure from senior management to measure results. This pressure can be a direct requirement to measure program effectiveness or a subtle expression of concern about the accountability of programs and processes.

Extremely low investments in measurement and evaluation. As indicated earlier, most organizations spend about 1 percent of their budget on measurement and evaluation processes. Investments significantly lower than this amount may indicate that there is little, if any, measurement or evaluation taking place, signaling the need for greater accountability. Expenditures in the 3–5 percent range indicate that learning and development and HR functions are undergoing serious evaluation.

Recent program disasters. Every organization has experienced situations in which a major program was implemented unsuccessfully. When there are multiple program failures, the function owning the programs often bears direct responsibility—or at least is assigned the blame. These failures may prompt the implementation of measurement and evaluation processes to determine the impact of programs, or, more appropriately, to forecast ROI prior to implementation.

A new director or leader in the function. A new leader often serves as a catalyst for change and may initiate a review of previous programs' success rates. These individuals do not have the stigma of ownership or attachment to old programs and are willing to take an objective view. However, the desire to gain an immediate gauge of program effectiveness may lead to impatience, if an evaluation process is not already in place.

Managers' desire to build cutting-edge functions. Some managers strive to create cutting-edge functions. In doing so, they may automatically build comprehensive measurement and evaluation processes in the overall strategy. These managers often set the pace for measurement and evaluation by highlighting the fact that they are serious about bringing accountability to their functions. These functions have formal guidelines around their measurement processes and build evaluation into program development. They often begin with thorough needs assessments to determine the best solutions, and then they monitor the progress of the programs and determine the business impact.

Lack of management support. In some cases, the image of a function suffers to the point that management no longer supports its efforts. While the unsatisfactory image may be caused by a number of factors, increased accountability often focuses on improving systems and processes, thereby shoring up the department's image.

Table 2 provides a self-check to determine your organization's candidacy for ROI implementation. Assess your readiness for ROI.

Table 2. ROI Readiness Self-Check

Is Your Organization a Candidate for ROI Implementation?

Check the most appropriate level of agreement for each statement; then total your score. Compare your score to the rubric on the next page.
1 = Strongly Disagree; 5 = Strongly Agree

	1	2	3	4	5
1. My organization is considered a large organization with a wide variety of programs.	☐	☐	☐	☐	☐
2. We have a large budget that attracts the interest of senior management.	☐	☐	☐	☐	☐
3. Our organization has a culture of measurement and is focused on establishing a variety of measures in all functions and departments.	☐	☐	☐	☐	☐
4. My organization is undergoing significant change.	☐	☐	☐	☐	☐
5. There is pressure from senior management to measure results of our programs.	☐	☐	☐	☐	☐
6. My function currently has a very low investment in measurement and evaluation.	☐	☐	☐	☐	☐
7. My organization has experienced more than one program disaster in the past.	☐	☐	☐	☐	☐
8. My department has a new leader.	☐	☐	☐	☐	☐
9. My team would like to be the leaders in our field.	☐	☐	☐	☐	☐
10. The image of our department is less than satisfactory.	☐	☐	☐	☐	☐
11. My clients are demanding that our processes show bottomline results.	☐	☐	☐	☐	☐
12. My function competes with other functions within our organization for resources.	☐	☐	☐	☐	☐
13. There is increased focus on linking our process to the strategic direction of the organization.	☐	☐	☐	☐	☐
14. My function is a key player in change initiatives currently taking place in the organization.	☐	☐	☐	☐	☐
15. Our overall budget is growing, and we are required to prove the bottomline value of our processes.	☐	☐	☐	☐	☐

Scoring

If you scored:

15–30	You are not yet a candidate for ROI.
31–45	You are not a strong candidate for ROI; however, it is time to start pursuing some type of measurement process.
46–60	You are a candidate for building skills to implement the ROI process. At this point, there is no real pressure to show the ROI, which is the perfect opportunity to perfect the process within the organization.
61–75	You should already be implementing a comprehensive measurement and evaluation process, including ROI.

CHAPTER 2: THE EVALUATION PUZZLE

Developing a credible and comprehensive measurement and evaluation process is much like putting together a puzzle. Five critical pieces come together to complete this puzzle, as shown in Figure 1.

The first piece of the puzzle is the *evaluation framework*. This framework serves as a way to categorize data describing the chain of impact that occurs as organizations invest in programs and projects. The second piece of the puzzle is the *ROI process model*. A process model is critical in that it depicts systematic steps to ensure consistent application of the evaluation methodology. The third piece of the evaluation puzzle is *operating standards* or *guiding principles*. These standards build credibility into the process by supporting a systematic methodology and conservative approach to program evaluation. Standards and guiding principles also support consistency in the process, helping to ensure that the data captured in the framework are reliable. The fourth piece of the evaluation puzzle is *case application and practice*. Case studies show real-world applications of the process and provide support for implementation. The final piece of the puzzle, *implementation*, brings together the other four pieces to implement the ROI Methodology. Critical elements of implementation, which will be discussed later, ensure that the evaluation process is fully integrated into the organization; that the organization develops the appropriate skills, procedures, and guidelines; and that a comprehensive communication strategy is in place so that the process is used to its fullest while maintaining credibility with key stakeholders. It is through successful implementation that an organization can achieve a positive ROI on its ROI practice.

Figure 1. Evaluation Puzzle

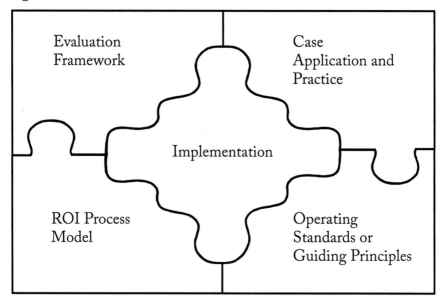

Together, these five pieces of the evaluation puzzle form a comprehensive measurement and evaluation system that contains a balanced set of measures, generates reliable data, and provides credible evidence of program success. The remainder of this book explains the pieces of the evaluation puzzle that make up the ROI Methodology.

Evaluation Framework

The first piece of the evaluation puzzle is the evaluation framework. An important contribution to the field of training measurement and evaluation is the work of Donald Kirkpatrick. In the 1950s, Kirkpatrick developed what was originally referred to as "four steps to evaluation."

ATD subsequently wrote a series of articles describing this concept. What was originally referred to as a series of steps has evolved into what is now a series of levels, with the help of Jack J. Phillips. In his seminal work, *Handbook of Training Evaluation and Measurement Methods* (1983), Phillips redefines the levels and adds ROI to the framework, resulting in what is now known as the "five-level evaluation framework." Users of the levels grew exponentially following this publication, and usage increased even more when Phillips partnered with ATD to develop the first in a series of case study books describing actual application of the five-level evaluation framework and ROI process model in 1994 (Phillips, 1994). During the same time frame, Kirkpatrick published his concept in the book *Evaluating Training Programs: The Four Levels* (1994).

Kirkpatrick Four-Level Framework

Table 3 presents Kirkpatrick's four levels and their respective definitions. The first of Kirkpatrick's four levels is Reaction, a measure of participant reaction to the program. Level 2, Learning, is the measure of changes in participants' attitudes, knowledge, or skills as a result of the program. Kirkpatrick defines Level 3, Behavior, as the measure of change in behavior on the job after attending the program. Kirkpatrick's fourth level, Results, measures changes in business results, such as productivity, quality, costs, sales, turnover, and higher profits (Kirkpatrick 1994).

Kirkpatrick's work provides the initial framework for evaluating learning and performance improvement programs. However, the most common measure for value-added benefits in other operational functions is ROI (Horngren 1982; Anthony and Reece 1983). As presented earlier, ROI is the comparison of earnings (net benefits) to investment (costs) (Kearsley 1982).

Table 3. Kirkpatrick's Four-Level Evaluation Framework

Level	Brief Description
Reaction	Measures participant reaction to the program
Learning	Measures the extent to which participants change attitudes, improve knowledge, and/or increase skills
Behavior	Measures the extent to which change in behavior occurs
Results	Measures changes in business results

Phillips Five-Level Framework

In order to address the need to show financial contribution to the organization while balancing the data with the additional measures, Jack J. Phillips expanded Kirkpatrick's four levels to add a fifth level, ROI (Phillips, 1983), and redefined the levels to address specific measures taken and questions answered through the measurement process. In addition, he provided the process model and standards to support actual application of evaluation at each level, taking the concept of levels further by adding methodology to support the collection and analysis of data. Table 4 illustrates Phillips' five-level evaluation framework.

The addition of Level 5, ROI, takes into account the steps in CBA and the calculation of the ROI percentage. In essence, it is bringing in an economic theory and new data not recognized in the original four steps. Where Kirkpatrick's fourth level stops at identifying improvement in business measures that occur after a program (Level 4, Results), Phillips' Level 4 includes a step to isolate that improvement to the program, accounting for other factors that may have also contributed. This step ensures an accurate accounting of program benefits (Phillips, 1996a). Then, to move from Level 4 to Level 5, the improvement in impact data is annualized, converted to monetary value, and compared to the fully loaded cost of the program (Phillips, 1996b). This process adds a new and different type of data and represents a new theoretical model, CBA; hence, it provides a new level to the framework.

In an effort to reposition program costs as investments, the five-level framework has been adapted to include Level 0, Input (Phillips and Phillips, 2007). This addition does not reflect a new level of evaluation results. It represents the activities that drive results. Program costs (Level 0 data) have always existed, in that they represent the program or project activities and all associated costs. The five levels of evaluation include all possible types of results that occur from a program. Level 0 does, however, represent the investment that organizations make in programs. This level of activity is the starting point of the chain of impact that occurs as people are involved in programs.

Table 4. Phillips' Five-Level Evaluation Framework

Level	Measurement Focus	Key Questions Answered
Investment		
0 Input	Describes the investment requirements	How many people are involved in the process? What is the per-person investment? What activities make up the investment?
Five Levels of Results		
1 Reaction and Planned Action	Measures participant satisfaction with the program or process and captures planned actions	Is the program or process relevant, important, useful, and helpful to the participant and the job environment?
2 Learning	Measures changes in knowledge, skills, and attitudes	Did participants increase or enhance knowledge, skills, or perceptions? Do they understand the information shared? Do they have the confidence to do what they need to do?
3 Application and Implementation	Measures changes in performance or action	Are participants applying the knowledge/skills/information? If yes, what is supporting them? If no, why not?
4 Business Impact	Measures changes in key business measures	How does the application improve output, quality, cost, time, and satisfaction? How do we know it was the program that caused this improvement?
5 ROI	Compares the program benefits to the costs	Do the monetary benefits of the program exceed the investment in the program?

Kirkpatrick, Phillips, and Cost-Benefit Analysis (CBA)

Table 5 provides a comparison of Kirkpatrick's framework, Phillips' framework, and the CBA process. As shown in Table 5, both Kirkpatrick and Phillips address participant reaction as well as learning and application of skills and behavior change. Level 4 (Impact/Results) is comparable to the identification of benefits in CBA; however, Phillips' framework is the only one of the three that addresses the issue of accounting for other influences. Level 5, ROI, includes the CBA steps to convert data to monetary value and to tabulate the fully loaded program costs. Kirkpatrick, Phillips, and CBA all consider the intangible benefits of implementing a program.

Table 5. Evaluation Frameworks Compared to Cost-Benefit Analysis

	Kirkpatrick's Four Levels	Phillips' Five Levels	CBA
Measure Participant Reaction	X	X	
Measure Learning	X	X	
Measure Application/Behavior	X	X	
Measure Impact/Results	X	X	X
Measure ROI		X	X
Isolate the Effects of the Program		X	
Determine Cost		X	X
Convert Benefits to Monetary Value		X	X
Identify Intangible Benefits	X	X	X

Although this distinction between the frameworks is important, it is necessary to note that not all programs should be evaluated at all five levels. Perhaps the best explanation for this is that, as the level of evaluation increases, so does its difficulty and expense. It takes time and resources to evaluate programs to the higher levels, so it is not feasible to do it for every program. Table 6 suggests targets for evaluating programs at different levels, based on the number and type of programs at the typical large organization.

Table 6. Suggested Evaluation Targets

Evaluation Levels	Percent of Programs to Evaluate at Each Level
Level 1 Reaction	90 – 100%
Level 2 Learning	60 – 80%
Level 3 Application	30 – 50%
Level 4 Impact	10 – 20%
Level 5 ROI	5 – 10%

Some programs should be evaluated just for reaction, some just for learning, etc. Programs are selected for evaluation at the Impact and ROI levels using criteria such as these:

- Expected program life cycle

- Importance of the program in meeting the organization's goals

- Cost of the program

- Visibility of the program

- Size of the target audience

- Extent of management interest

However, when evaluating at a higher level, it is important to evaluate at lower levels as well. A chain of impact occurs as participants react and plan action (Level 1) based on the knowledge, skills, and information acquired during the program (Level 2), which are then applied on the job (Level 3), resulting in improvement in business measures (Level 4). When a Level 5 ROI evaluation is planned, evaluation should be conducted at all levels; if measurements are not taken at each of these levels, it is difficult to:

- conclude that the results achieved are actually a result of the program;

- explain how results at the higher levels were achieved;

- provide relevant information to every stakeholder; and

- improve results based on an evidence-based breakdown in program implementation.

ROI Process Model

The second piece of the evaluation puzzle is the ROI process model. The ROI model shows the systematic steps to ensure that the evaluation methodology is implemented consistently. Replicability of the evaluation process is imperative. A step-by-step model will ensure that this replication takes place according to a systematic approach. Figure 2 shows the ROI Methodology process model. The model consists of four stages: Evaluation Planning, Data Collection, Data Analysis, and Reporting. The model will be explored in the next two chapters.

Figure 2. The ROI Methodology Process Model

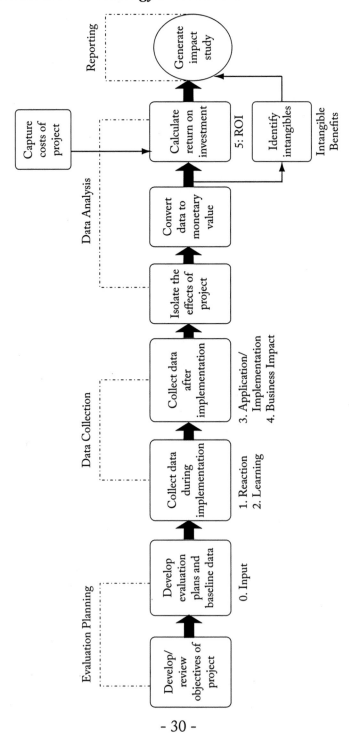

Operating Standards: Guiding Principles

Operating standards, the third piece of the evaluation puzzle, also help with replication, as standards ensure that there is consistency in the evaluation process and that a conservative approach is taken. Standards or guiding principles keep the evaluation credible and help ensure that data captured in the framework are reliable. When implementing ROI, there are 12 Guiding Principles to use as operating standards:

1. **Tell the Complete Story of Program Success**
    When conducting a higher level of evaluation, collect data at lower levels. ROI is a critical measure, but it is only one of the measures necessary to explain the full impact of a program, so lower levels of data must be included in the analysis. The data at the lower levels also provide important information that can be helpful in making adjustments for future program implementation.

2. **Conserve Resources for Higher-Level Evaluations**
    When conducting a higher-level evaluation, do not be so comprehensive at the lower levels. Lower-level measures are critical in telling the complete story and cannot be omitted. However, shortcuts can be taken to conserve resources. For example, when the client is interested in business impact, shortcuts can be taken at Levels 2 and 3.

3. **Use the Most Credible Sources**
    When collecting and analyzing data, use only the most credible sources. Credibility is the most important factor in the measurement and evaluation process. Without it, the results are meaningless. Collecting data from the most credible sources will enhance the perception of the quality and accuracy of data analysis and results. The key is in defining a credible source. Credibility lies in how much the source knows about the measure and what influences improvement in the measures. Participants are often that most

credible source, but it may be helpful to balance their perspective with input from another and equally credible source.

4. **Choose the Most Conservative Alternative**

   When analyzing data, select the most conservative alternative for calculations. This principle is at the heart of the evaluation process. A conservative approach lowers the ROI and helps to build the needed credibility with the target audience. It also ensures reliable comparisons of data from program to program.

5. **Give Credit Where Credit Is Due**

   Use at least one method to isolate the effects of the solution. This step is imperative. Without some method to isolate the effects of the program, the evaluation results are considered inaccurate and overstated. While a control group arrangement is the classic technique, it is not always a feasible option, so there are alternatives. This guiding principle requires consideration of those other techniques.

6. **Make No Assumptions for Non-Respondents**

   If no improvement data are available for a population or from a specific source, assume that no improvement has occurred. If participants do not provide data—if they are no longer a part of the organization or they perform a different function—assume that little or no improvement has occurred. Inferring benefits for which there is no basis overstates the results, thereby risking credibility and reliability. This ultraconservative approach further enhances the credibility of the results and allows for comparison of program evaluation output.

7. **Adjust Estimates for Error**

   Adjust estimates of improvement for the potential error in the estimates. This guideline contributes to the conservative approach of the process. Using estimates is very common in reporting data, including financial and cost-benefit information. To enhance the credibility of estimated data used in ROI evaluation of learning and performance improvement programs, estimates are weighted with a level of confidence, adjusting the estimate for potential error.

8. **Omit the Extremes**

   Extreme data items and unsupported claims should not be used in ROI calculations. Again, to maintain credibility of the results, steps should be taken to be conservative in the analysis. For example, if you have a list of numbers all ranging from 30 to 70 and only one 100, that 100 would be considered an outlier or extreme data item. Extreme data items can skew results to the low side as well as the high side. Omitting extreme data items from the analysis eliminates their influence on the results.

9. **Report First-Year Benefits Only for Short-Term Programs**

   Use only the first year of annual benefits in the ROI analysis of short-term solutions. If benefits are not quickly realized for most learning and performance improvement programs, they are probably not worth the cost. Therefore, the ROI for short-term programs should be based on first-year benefits rather than inflating the results by assuming benefits will continue in future years. For more extensive programs, where implementation spans several months or more, assuming benefits for multiple years may be appropriate.

10. **Account for All Program Costs**

    Fully load costs of the solution when analyzing ROI. All costs of the program are tabulated, beginning with the cost of the needs analysis and ending with the cost of the evaluation. As part of the conservative approach, the costs are loaded to ensure a more credible and reliable ROI.

11. **Report Intangible Benefits**

    Define intangible measures as measures that are purposely not converted to monetary values. While the ROI is the ultimate measure of program success, it is important to report the intangible benefits. Intangible benefits such as customer satisfaction, employee engagement, better teamwork, and innovation are also important measures of program success. Sometimes the intangibles carry as much weight with senior executives as a program's financial benefits.

12. Communicate and Use Evaluation Data

Communicate results from the ROI Methodology to all key stakeholders. The purpose of evaluating programs using the ROI Methodology is to report success, gain respect, influence decisions, and improve programs. If evaluation results are not reported and used, then evaluation becomes just another activity, which will represent a cost that can be cut. Just as with your programs, ensure that your evaluation practice is positioned as an investment.

Table 7 summarizes these guiding principles. Collectively, these standards ensure that the evaluation approach is conservative and that the impact study can be replicated, making them a crucial part of the puzzle. They also ensure that the ROI for programs such as learning and development, performance improvement, and HR can be compared to the ROI of operational processes and initiatives in the organization.

Table 7. Twelve Guiding Principles

Operating Standards / Guiding Principles

Guiding Principle	Meaning
1. When conducting a higher-level evaluation, collect data at lower levels.	Tell the complete story of program success.
2. When conducting a higher-level evaluation, do not be so comprehensive at the lower levels.	Conserve resources for the higher-level evaluations.
3. When collecting and analyzing data, use only the most credible sources.	Use the most credible sources.
4. When analyzing data, select the most conservative alternative for calculations.	Choose the most conservative alternative.
5. Use at least one method to isolate the effects of the solution.	Give credit where credit is due.
6. If no improvement data are available for a population or from a specific source, assume that no improvement has occurred.	Make no assumptions for non-respondents.
7. Adjust estimates of improvement for the potential error in the estimates.	Adjust estimates for error.
8. Extreme data items and unsupported claims should not be used in ROI calculations.	Omit the extremes.
9. Use only the first year of annual benefits in the ROI analysis of short-term solutions	Report only first year benefits for short-term programs.
10. Fully load costs of the solution when analyzing ROI.	Account for all program costs.
11. Define intangible measures as measures that are purposely not converted to monetary values.	Report intangible benefits.
12. Communicate results from the ROI Methodology to all key stakeholders.	Communicate and use your evaluation data.

Case Application and Practice

Another piece of the evaluation puzzle is the development of case studies by the various functions to show success, promote programs, or justify new programs. Case studies from other organizations can serve as benchmarks or examples of success. Those within similar industries provide even better benchmarks, because they address similar issues and target similar concerns. Case studies from a global perspective provide evidence of success with the ROI Methodology in a variety of organizations and industries, supporting the need to pursue comprehensive measurement and evaluation. Case studies also serve as learning aids for practitioners, managers, and executives who are developing capability in measurement and evaluation.

While the use of case studies from other organizations is helpful in understanding the merits of ROI implementation and the success of specific programs, studies developed by the implementing organization are more powerful. These case studies describe the success of programs that are directly beneficial to the organization. They also provide evidence that the organization is putting theory into practice rather than relying on theory alone. Table 8 provides the output of a few published case studies.

Table 8. Sample Case Studies

Measuring the ROI:	Key Impact Measures:	ROI
Sales Training (Verizon)	Net adds	113%[1]
Engagement Initiative (Home Furnishings Company)	Sales, voluntary turnover, compliance, customer complaints	210%[2]
Electronic Documentation Tool (Caremark/CVS Pharmacy Operations)	Productivity, quality, materials cost	79.5%[3]
Employee Retraining (Codelco)	Dispatch and power view indicators	115%[3]
E-Learning (Petroleum Company)	Sales	206%[4]
Internal Graduate Degree Program (Federal Agency)	Retention, individual graduate projects	153%[5]
Executive Coaching (International Hotel Chain)	Several measures, including productivity, quality, cost control, and product development time	221%[6]
Sales Training (Tata Sky Ltd.)	Various measures—at least two per manager	311%[6]

[1]   *Human Capital Analytics @ Work Volume 2.* Patti P. Phillips and Rebecca L. Ray. New York: The Conference Board, 2017.

[2]   *Measuring the Success of Employee Engagement.* Patti P. Phillips and Jack J. Phillips. Alexandria, VA: ATD Press, 2016.

[3]   *ROI in Action Casebook.* Patti P. Phillips and Jack J. Phillips. San Francisco, CA: Pfeiffer, 2008.

[4]   *Measuring the Success of Learning Through Technology.* Tamar Elkeles, Patti P. Phillips, and Jack J. Phillips. Alexandria, VA: ASTD Press, 2014.

[5]   *In Action: Measuring ROI in the Public Sector.* Patti P. Phillips, Editor. Alexandria, VA: ASTD Press, 2002.

[6]   *Measuring the Success of Coaching.* Patti P. Phillips, Jack J. Phillips, and Lisa Edwards. Alexandria, VA: ASTD Press, 2012.

Implementation

The final piece of the evaluation puzzle is implementation. The best tool, technique, or model will not be successful unless it is properly utilized and becomes a routine part of the function. As with any change, the people affected by the implementation of a comprehensive measurement and evaluation process, including the staff and other stakeholders, will likely resist it. Part of that resistance will be based on realistic barriers. Part of it, however, will be based on misunderstandings and perceived problems. In both cases, the organization must work to overcome resistance by carefully and methodically implementing ROI evaluation using the following critical steps:

1. Assign responsibilities
2. Develop skills
3. Develop an implementation plan
4. Prepare or revise evaluation guidelines
5. Brief managers on the evaluation process

Assign Responsibilities

To ensure successful ROI implementation, assign responsibilities up front—before implementation begins. Who will lead the evaluation effort? Will evaluation be integrated into the function, or will the evaluation leader report to the chief financial officer (CFO)? Is it more appropriate to contract with a third-party evaluation provider and have only an internal coordinator? These questions and others must be considered when implementing any evaluation strategy.

Develop Skills

Another key step in successful implementation is the development of skills and capabilities. A complete understanding of each step in the evaluation process will simplify implementation, reducing the stress and frustration often associated with jumping from one process to another.

Develop an Implementation Plan

Planning for implementation will save time and money. By using a basic set of criteria to review existing programs as well as proposed new programs, the staff can develop an implementation plan. This plan will assist in determining which programs will be evaluated at which levels (by using the criteria discussed earlier) and how the necessary resources will be allocated.

Along with an implementation plan to select programs for different levels of evaluation, there should also be a project plan to help to manage the overall evaluation process. From a practical standpoint, this project plan serves to support the transition from the present situation to a desired future state.

Implementation plans typically include the following ten steps:

1. **Review existing programs, processes, reports, and data.** This step is essential to understanding past practices and how to incorporate the new methodology most effectively.

2. **Develop skills.** Developing the skills necessary to implement the ROI Methodology is essential for complete integration into the learning and development, performance improvement, or HR process.

3. **Finalize evaluation planning documents.** The planning documents necessary to implement the ROI Methodology are critical to ensure that every step of the process is taken and that key stakeholders agree with those steps.

4. **Collect evaluation data.** This step represents the data collection process.

5. **Analyze evaluation data.** This step represents the time necessary to analyze the data after collection.

6. **Develop reports.** As we will discuss in Chapter 4, developing a variety of reports helps to address specific audience needs. Of course, a complete impact study will be produced, but after the executive management understands the evaluation process, a brief summary (in some cases, a single summary page will suffice) will be an appropriate method to communicate results.

7. **Present impact study results.** Different audiences need different information. In the initial implementation of the ROI Methodology, results should be presented in a formal setting to ensure clear communication of the process itself. Presentation of results to staff members may take place in a less formal setting, such as a weekly staff meeting.

8. **Develop a scorecard framework.** Sometimes it is important to show the results of an entire function. Unless ROI is calculated for all programs, it is not possible to show one ROI for the entire function. However, a scorecard allows the function or department to roll up data from all evaluations to show a macro-level view of success.

9. **Develop guidelines.** As the ROI Methodology is implemented and integrated into various functions and processes, guidelines are developed to ensure consistent and long-term implementation.

10. **Brief managers.** Management understanding of the evaluation process is critical. Managers who are not involved in a particular evaluation project might still be interested in the process. Manager briefings are a way to communicate not only the results of the evaluation but the process in general. Each individual program evaluation will have individual project plans to detail the steps necessary to complete the project as well as to keep the evaluation project on track. Planning is the key to successful ROI implementation.

Table 9 provides a sample project plan.

Table 9. Simple ROI Implementation Plan

PROJECT PLAN

	Oct	Nov	Dec	Jan	Feb	Mar	Apr	May	Jun	Jul	Aug	Sep
1. Review of Existing Programs, Processes, Reports, Data	■	■										
2. Develop Skills			■									
3. Finalize Evaluation Planning Documents			■	■								
4. Collect Evaluation Data				■	■	■	■	■	■			
5. Analyze Evaluation Data									■	■	■	
6. Develop Reports											■	
7. Present Impact Study Results												■
8. Develop Scorecard Framework									■	■	■	■
9. Develop Guidelines				■	■	■	■	■	■	■		
10. Brief Managers												

Prepare or Revise Evaluation Guidelines

Guidelines keep the implementation process on track. A clear set of guidelines helps to ensure that the process continues as designed in the event of changes in staff or management. They also establish the evaluation process as an integral part of the overall learning and performance improvement strategy.

Brief Managers on the Evaluation Process

Communicating to managers about the evaluation process will help to enlist their support during the implementation process. The unknown can often become a barrier, so if the organization makes the effort to explain each step, it is more likely that managers will understand and support the evaluation effort.

All five of the pieces of the evaluation puzzle are necessary to build a comprehensive measurement and evaluation process. The next two chapters describe the ROI Methodology step by step.

CHAPTER 3: THE ROI METHODOLOGY

An effective ROI methodology must balance many issues, including feasibility, simplicity, credibility, and soundness, in part to satisfy the needs and requirements of three major target audiences. First, staff members who use the process must have a clear, straightforward approach. Otherwise, the process may appear confusing and complex, causing many staff members to assume that it is impossible, or at a minimum too expensive, to develop the ROI for programs. If staff members perceive the ROI Methodology as inconceivable, many will give up.

Second, the ROI Methodology must meet the unique requirements of the clients—those who request and approve programs. Clients need a process that will provide quantitative and qualitative results. They need a process that will develop a calculation similar to the ROI formula applied to other types of investment, and a process that reflects their frame of reference, background, and level of understanding. More importantly, they need a process with which they can identify—one that is sound, realistic, and practical enough to earn their confidence.

Finally, the process needs the support of researchers. The process must hold up under their scrutiny and close examination. Researchers want to use models, formulas, assumptions, and theories that are sound and based on commonly accepted practices. They also want a process that produces accurate values and consistent outcomes and that can be replicated reliably from one situation to another. If two different practitioners are evaluating a program, the process should result in the same measurements.

Criteria for an Effective ROI Process

An ROI process must adhere to certain criteria in order to meet the critical challenges of those who will be using it. The following criteria came out of working with learning and development, performance improvement, and HR managers and specialists to develop comprehensive measurement and evaluation processes within their organizations.

Simple

An ROI process must be simple—devoid of complex formulas, lengthy equations, and complicated methodologies. Most ROI models do not meet these criteria. In an attempt to obtain statistical perfection, many ROI models and processes are too complex to understand and use. Consequently, they are not implemented. While there is merit in striving for statistical accuracy, if a model is so complicated that it cannot be used, the organization does not stand to benefit from it.

Economical

An ROI process must be economical and easily implemented. While the initial implementation of any new methodology can be costly, once that methodology is integrated into the organization and has become a routine part of the process, only minimal additional resources should be required to sustain its implementation.

Credible

The assumptions, methodology, and outcomes of the evaluation process must be credible. Logical, methodical steps earn the respect of practitioners, senior managers, and researchers. This requires not only a theoretically sound process but also a process that is practical in its approach.

Theoretically Sound

From a research perspective, an ROI methodology must be theoretically sound and based on generally accepted practices. Unfortunately, this requirement can lead to an extensive, complicated process. Ideally, the process must strike a balance between maintaining a practical, sensible approach and ensuring a sound theoretical basis for the procedures. This is perhaps one of the greatest challenges to those who develop models for ROI measurement.

Accounts for Other Factors

An ROI process must account for other factors that influence output measures targeted by the program. This is one of the most often-overlooked issues, but it is necessary to build credibility and accuracy within the process. The ROI process should pinpoint the program's contribution while considering all other influences.

Appropriate

An ROI process should be appropriate for a variety of programs. Some models apply only to a small number of programs, such as those focused on productivity improvement. Ideally, the process must be applicable to every type of program, from career development and organizational development to major change initiatives. It is not practical for an organization to need a different evaluation process for every type of program.

Flexible

An ROI process must have the flexibility to be applied on a pre-program basis as well as a post-program basis. In some situations, an estimate of the ROI is required before developing the actual program. The process should be flexible enough to adjust to a range of potential time frames for calculating ROI.

Applicable

An ROI process must be applicable with both hard and soft data. Hard data are typically represented as output, quality, cost, and time.

Soft data include job satisfaction, customer satisfaction, absenteeism, turnover, grievances, and complaints.

Considers All Costs

An ROI process must include all the fully loaded costs associated with programs. These costs include: the initial needs assessment; development; delivery, including facilitator, facility, and participant; and evaluation. Although the term ROI is frequently loosely used to express any of the benefits of a program, an acceptable ROI process compares the monetary benefits of a program to all program costs. Omitting or understating program costs will overstate the ROI and thus destroy its credibility.

Successful Track Record

Finally, an ROI process needs a successful track record with a variety of types of applications. In far too many situations, models are created that might look good but that are never applied successfully. An effective measurement and evaluation process should withstand the wear and tear of implementation and prove valuable to users. To be worthwhile for an organization, an ROI process should meet the vast majority, if not all, of these criteria. The bad news, however, is that most models do not. Table 10 provides a checklist that is useful when evaluating processes against the criteria.

Table 10. Criteria for a Credible ROI Process

How Does Your Measurement and Evaluation Process Compare?

Criteria	ROI Methodology	Balanced Scorecard	Economic Value Added	Other	Other
Simple	X				
Economical	X				
Credible	X				
Theoretically sound	X				
Accounts for other factors	X				
Appropriate with a variety of programs	X				
Applicable on pre-program and post-program basis	X				
Measures both hard and soft data	X				
Includes all fully loaded costs	X				
Successful track record	X				

The ROI Methodology

The ROI Methodology developed by Dr. Jack J. Phillips and described in this book is shown in Figure 2 (see page 30). It meets the standards and criteria described above and provides a balanced approach to evaluating all types of programs and initiatives. The process generates five levels of results: reaction and planned action (Level 1); learning (Level 2); application and implementation (Level 3); business impact (Level 4); and ROI (Level 5). In addition, business impact measures that are not converted to money are reported as a sixth type of data—these are the intangibles.

The process is divided into four stages. The first stage includes *evaluation planning*. This step begins with the development of program objectives and comprehensive evaluation plans. The second stage represents *data collection*. Data are collected from different sources at different time frames to develop a balance of measures. The third stage of the process is *data analysis*. At this stage, the practitioners isolate the program from other influences, convert data to monetary value, tabulate program costs, and calculate the ROI. It is also at this stage that the intangible benefits, those benefits not converted to monetary value, are identified. The final stage of the process is *reporting*. This last step in this comprehensive process, reporting results, is vital, as it is during this stage that program owners demonstrate the success of their programs. It is also at this stage when program owners and other stakeholders make decisions about program improvement, program expansion, or program elimination. The next chapter explores reporting in more detail.

Evaluation Planning

The first stage of the ROI Methodology, evaluation planning, establishes the foundation for success with the other stages. Thorough planning ensures that the evaluation addresses the appropriate objectives and utilizes the appropriate data collection instruments and that the client agrees on data analysis procedures. The evaluation planning stage includes two steps: developing program objectives and developing the evaluation plan.

Develop Program Objectives
Before ROI evaluation begins, it is important to achieve clarity on the program objectives. These objectives form the basis for determining the depth of the evaluation, meaning that they determine what level of evaluation will take place. Program objectives range from participant reaction to the actual ROI target. Program objectives link directly to the results of the front-end analysis or needs assessment. Figure 3 demonstrates the alignment between needs, objectives, and evaluation. As shown, the needs assessment process begins with identifying the potential payoff or opportunity for an organization or function (Level

5 Payoff Needs). With this in mind, the business needs are then identi-fied (Level 4 Business Needs). A thorough needs analysis follows to identify the performance needs (Level 3 Performance Needs) that, if addressed, will help address the business needs as well. The knowledge, skills, and information needed to achieve the desired performance are identified (Level 2 Learning Needs), taking into consideration the par-ticipants' preferences for learning (Level 1 Preference Needs). For each of these levels of need, it is necessary to develop objectives and then to link those objectives to levels of evaluation. This will ensure that the right questions are asked during the evaluation process. This process of alignment ensures that programs are positioned for success and that the evaluation process considers the appropriate measures.

Figure 3. Business Alignment Model

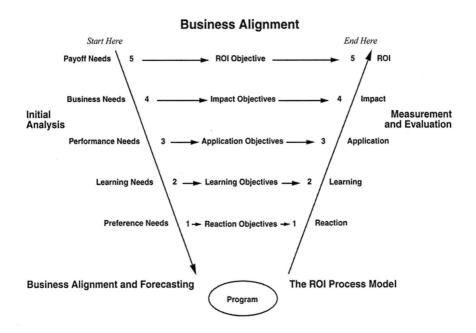

Table 11 shows an example of how the alignment process comes to-gether for a particular program. To check your understanding of the five-level framework and how objectives relate to the framework, com-plete the exercise on page 51.

Table 11. Example of Alignment

Sample Linkage Between Needs, Objectives, and Evaluation

Level	Needs	Objectives	Evaluation
5	$1.6 million in costs due to falsely rejected syringes	25% ROI	• Program costs compared to monetary benefits of program • Monetary benefit determined by cost savings of reduced number of false rejects
4	False rejects are a problem; false rejects are defined as syringes rejected when they are actually usable	• Reduce the number of false rejects by 10% within six months	• Monitor false rejects for six months • Participant estimates used for isolation
3	Inspectors are incorrectly identifying syringes as unacceptable	• Follow the five-step process during 100% of inspections • Utilize job aid as needed • Identify barriers to following the five-step process	• Follow-up questionnaire to participants three months after the training to check frequency of skill application and barriers • Unscheduled audits over six months
2	Deficiency in skills to recognize unacceptable syringes	• Demonstrate the five-step process and ability to follow job aid • Know the difference between acceptable and unacceptable syringes • Describe the consequences of incorrectly categorizing syringes	• Demonstrate ability to identify acceptable and unacceptable syringes • Indicate knowledge and understanding by completing learning assessment

1	One-day workshop and introduction to new job aid	• Program receives favorable rating of 4 out of 5 on the following:
		  ◦ Relevance of workshop content and job aid
		  ◦ Importance of following the five-step inspection process
		  ◦ Intent to use job aid during inspections
		  ◦ Other measures important to design and delivery of content
			• Reaction questionnaire administered at the end of the workshop

Exercise: Matching Objectives with Levels of Evaluation

Instructions: For each objective listed below, indicate the level of evaluation at which the objective is aimed.

    Level 1 – Reaction and Planned Action
    Level 2 – Learning
    Level 3 – Application and Implementation
    Level 4 – Business Impact
    Level 5 – Return on Investment

Objective	Evaluation Level
1. Decrease error rates on reports by 20% within three months of the program	————
2. Increase the use of disciplinary discussion skills in 90% of situations where work habits are unacceptable	————
3. Achieve a post-test score increase of 30% over pre-test	————
4. Within six weeks of completing the course, initiate at least three cost reduction projects as defined in the action plan	————
5. Decrease the amount of time required to complete a project within three months of learning the software	————
6. Achieve a 2:1 benefit-to-cost ratio one year after program implementation	————
7. Receive an instructor rating from participants of at least 4.5 out of 5	————
8. Increase the external customer satisfaction index by 25% in three months	————
9. Handle customer complaints with the five-step process in 95% of complaint situations	————
10. At least 50% of participants use all customer interaction skills with every customer	————

Answers:

(1) L-4; (2) L-3; (3) L-2; (4) L-3; (5) L-4; (6) L-5; (7) L-1; (8) L-4; (9) L-3; (10) L-3

Develop Evaluation Plan

After defining program objectives, the next step is to develop the evaluation plan. This plan helps ensure that each step of the evaluation process is addressed appropriately. As shown in Tables 12 and 13, the actual evaluation planning documents address each step of the process. The steps in the planning process include developing both a detailed data collection plan and a data analysis plan. The data collection plan begins with broad program objectives. Next, more specificity is given to those objectives as the practitioner defines the specific measures and targets that indicate success with the objectives. Determining how to evaluate each objective up front will save time and eliminate confusion later. The next steps include determining how to collect the data and from what sources to obtain them. Practitioners determine the timing of the data collection during the initial planning stage as well as who will be responsible for gathering the data items from the various sources.

After developing the data collection plan, Level 4 data items are copied to the ROI analysis plan. In this phase of the planning process, practitioners decide on the methods for isolating the effects of the program and converting data to monetary value. Program cost categories are identified, as are the Level 4 business measures that will not be converted to monetary value—the intangible benefits. Other potential influences that may affect the identified business measures are also noted during this phase. Finally, the target audiences for the final results are identified.

Table 12. Data Collection Plan

Data Collection Plan

Program: _____   Responsibility: _____   Date: _____

Level	Broad Program Objective(s)	Measures	Data Collection Method/Instruments	Data Sources	Timing	Responsibilities
1	**Reaction and Planned Action**					
2	**Learning and Confidence**					
3	**Application and Implementation**					
4	**Business Impact**					
5	ROI					

Comments: _____

Table 13. ROI Analysis Plan

ROI Analysis Plan

Program: _____   Responsibility: _____   Date: _____

Data Items (Usually Level 4)	Methods for Isolating the Effects of the Program/Process	Methods of Converting Data to Monetary Values	Cost Categories	Intangible Benefits	Communication Targets for Final Report	Other Influences/ Issues During Application	Comments

Although much time and effort is put into this process, planning has many advantages:

- Planning provides a road map to complete the evaluation process.

- Agreeing up front with the client how the evaluation will take place will save frustration (for both parties) during the process.

- Presenting the plan to the program staff or project team, including program facilitators, will communicate expectations of program success and the process by which success will be measured. This step reinforces to the staff that the evaluation is a process-improvement tool rather than an individual performance evaluation.

- Communicating the evaluation plan to program participants will reaffirm the importance of the program. It will also prepare participants to provide appropriate data at the appropriate time. This not only helps to ensure that credible data are received but will also help to increase response rates during post-program follow-up.

Data Collection

The second stage of the ROI Methodology is data collection. Data are collected at two points—during and after program implementation. Data are collected during the program to measure participants' reactions and to determine their planned actions. In addition, learning is measured to determine the extent to which participants acquired the knowledge, skills, and information necessary to improve performance. These measures help to ensure that adjustments are made as needed to keep the program on track. They also provide evaluators and program owners with an initial indication of a program's potential success. For example, if participants indicate that the content is relevant to their jobs, and they appear to acquire the requisite knowledge, program owners can feel somewhat confident that participants will apply what they learned. If, however, participants indicate that the content is relevant to their jobs, but all learning assessments show that they do not "get it," then the program owner needs to consider a follow-up mechanism to support participants' acquisition of knowledge.

Data are also collected on a post-program basis. Practitioners gather information regarding the application of skills and knowledge as well as the impact that the program has had on the organization. These data are collected some time after the knowledge, skills, and information have begun to be applied routinely. Both hard data and soft data are collected using a variety of methods, such as the following:

- Attitudinal surveys

- Detailed questionnaires

- On-the-job observation

- Tests and assessments

- Interviews

- Focus groups

- Action plans

- Performance contracts

- Performance records

An important challenge in data collection is selecting the method or methods appropriate for the setting and the specific program, within the given time and budget constraints. Table 14 lists considerations for selecting data collection methods.

Table 14. Considerations When Selecting Data Collection Methods

When selecting data collection methods, consider the following:

- Type of data
    - Level of Evaluation
    - Quantitative Versus Qualitative
    - Financial Versus Intangible
- Time
    - Participant Time Required to Provide Data
    - Supervisor Time Required to Provide Data
- Costs
- Accuracy
    - Validity
    - Reliability
- Utility of Capturing Additional Data
- Organization Culture / Philosophy

Data Analysis

Data analysis is the third stage of the ROI Methodology. At this stage, the results of the program begin to become clear. By isolating the effects of the program, results are more accurate—there is minimal question as to how much of the results can actually be attributed to the program. Data conversion takes place so that program benefits can be converted to monetary value. The costs are tabulated, and the ROI calculation is developed, in this stage. Finally, the intangible benefits are identified. Each of these steps is presented in greater detail below.

Isolate the Effects of the Program
An often-overlooked issue in evaluating programs and projects is the process of isolating the effects of the program. There are several specific strategies that determine the amount of performance improvement directly related to the program. Isolating the effects is essential,

because many factors will influence performance data after the implementation of a program. The specific strategies in this step will pinpoint the amount of improvement directly related to the program. The result is increased accuracy and credibility of the ROI Methodology results. The following are some commonly used strategies to address this important issue:

- A pilot group of participants in a program is compared with a control group not participating in the program to isolate program impact.

- Trend lines are used to project the values of specific output, and projections are compared with the actual data after the program.

- A forecasting model uses mathematical relationships between input and output variables to project output measures influenced by the program under evaluation.

- Participants estimate the amount of improvement that is related to the program.

- Supervisors and managers estimate the impact of the program on the output measures.

- External studies provide input about the impact of the program.

- Independent experts provide estimates of the impact of the program on the performance variable.

- When feasible, other influencing factors are identified, and their impact is estimated or calculated, leaving the remaining unexplained improvement attributable to the program.

- Customers provide input about the extent to which the program has influenced their decisions to use a product or service.

Collectively, these strategies provide a comprehensive set of tools to address the critical issue of isolating the effects of programs and processes.

Convert Data to Monetary Values

To calculate the ROI, practitioners convert business impact data to monetary values and compare those values to program costs. This requires that a value be placed on each unit of data connected with the programs. The list below shows most of the key strategies used to convert data to monetary values. The specific strategy selected depends on the type of data and the situation:

- *Output data*, such as additional sales, are converted to profit contribution (or cost savings) and reported as a standard value.

- The cost of a *quality measure*, such as a customer complaint, is calculated and reported as a standard value.

- Employee *time saved* is converted to wages and benefits, a standard value.

- *Historical costs* of preventing a measure, such as a lost-time accident, are used when available.

- *Internal and external experts* estimate the value of a measure, such as an employee complaint.

- *External databases* contain the approximate value or cost of a data item, such as employee turnover.

- The measure is *linked to other measures* for which the costs are easily developed (e.g., employee satisfaction linked to turnover).

- *Participants estimate* the cost or value of the data item, such as work-group conflict.

- *Supervisors or managers estimate* costs or values, when they are willing and able (e.g., an unscheduled absence).

- The *program staff estimates* the value of a data item, such as a sexual harassment complaint.

Money tells a compelling story. Converting a measure to money quantifies the measure in meaningful terms. To calculate the ROI of a program, the conversion step is essential. However, even during the front analysis work, monetary values describe the opportunity and problems an organization faces in terms that are more specific. The process to convert measures to money can be challenging, particularly with soft data, but it can be accomplished methodically using one or more of these strategies.

Capture Program Costs

The next step in the data analysis stage is capturing program costs. Tabulating the costs involves monitoring or developing all costs related to the program. Costs related to programs include the following:

- Assessment

- Development

- Program materials

- Instructor/facilitator

- Facilities

- Travel/lodging/meals

- Participant salaries and benefits

- Administrative/overhead

- Evaluation

A fully loaded cost profile is recommended when tabulating all direct and indirect costs. Table 15 provides a sample cost summary detailing the fully loaded costs necessary to maintain a conservative ROI calculation. Here is a general rule of thumb when it comes to calculating program costs:

When in doubt, leave it in.

By accounting for the full cost of a program, not only do you demonstrate a high level of accountability, but you ensure that the ROI is credible.

Table 15. Fully Loaded Cost Profile

FULLY LOADED COST PROFILE

Analysis Costs

Salaries and employee benefits
  (No. of people x average salary x employee
  benefits factor x hours on project)   _____

Meals, travel, and incidental expenses   _____

Office supplies and expenses   _____

Printing and reproduction   _____

Outside services   _____

Equipment expenses   _____

Registration fees   _____

General overhead allocation   _____

Other miscellaneous expenses   _____

A. Total Analysis Costs   _____

Development Costs

Salaries and employee benefits
  (No. of people x average salary x employee
  benefits factor x hours on project)   _____

Meals, travel, and incidental expenses   _____

Office supplies and expenses   _____

Program materials and supplies   _____

Video recordings   _____

CDs/DVDs   _____

Artwork   _____

Manuals and materials   _____

Printing and reproduction   _____

Outside services   _____

Equipment expenses   _____

General overhead allocation   _____

Other miscellaneous expenses   _____

B. Total Development Costs   _____

Delivery Costs

Participant expenses   _____

Salaries and employee benefits
  (No. of people x average salary x employee
  benefits factor x time involved in the project)   _____

Instructor expenses   _____

Salaries and benefits   _____

Meals, travel, and incidental expenses   _____

Outside services   _____

Meals, travel, and accommodations
  (No. of participants x average daily expenses
  x days involved in the project)   _____

Program materials and supplies   _____

Participant replacement expenses (if applicable)   _____

Lost production (explain basis)   _____

Facility costs   _____

Facilities rental   _____

Facilities expenses allocation   _____

Equipment expenses   _____

General overhead allocation   _____

Other miscellaneous expenses   _____

C. Total Delivery Costs   _____

Evaluation Costs

Salaries and employee benefits
  (No. of people x average salary x employee
  benefits factor x hours on project)   _____

Meals, travel, and incidental expenses   _____

Participant expenses   _____

Office supplies and expenses   _____

Printing and reproduction   _____

Outside services   _____

Equipment expenses   _____

General overhead allocation   _____

Other miscellaneous expenses   _____

D. Total Evaluation Costs   _____

Total Program Costs (A + B + C + D)   _____

Calculate the Return on Investment (ROI)

As previously discussed, the return on investment is calculated by comparing the monetary benefits of a program to the costs. The BCR, a related measure, is the monetary benefits of the program divided by the costs. In formula form, it is this:

$$BCR = \frac{Program\ Benefits}{Program\ Costs}$$

The return on investment uses the *net* benefits divided by costs. The net benefits are program benefits minus the costs. In formula form, ROI becomes:

$$ROI = \frac{Net\ Program\ Benefits}{Program\ Costs} \times 100$$

This is the same basic formula commonly used to evaluate other investments where ROI is traditionally reported as earnings divided by investment.

The BCR and ROI present the same general information but with slightly different perspectives. For example, say an effective meeting-skills program produced a savings of $581,000 with a cost of $229,000. This would be the BCR:

$$BCR = \frac{\$581,000}{\$229,000} = 2.54\ (or\ 2.54{:}1)$$

As this calculation shows, every $1 invested in the program returned $2.54 in monetary benefits. However, to calculate ROI in this example, net benefits are $581,000 - $229,000 = $352,000. Thus, the ROI is this:

$$ROI\% = \frac{\$352,000}{\$229,000} \times 100 = 154\%$$

This means each $1 invested in the program returns approximately $1.54 in *net* benefits, after costs are covered. The benefits are usually expressed as annual benefits for short-term programs, representing the amount saved or gained for a complete year after the program has been implemented. Although the benefits may continue after the first year, the impact usually diminishes and is therefore omitted from calculations in short-term situations. For long-term projects, the benefits can be extrapolated for multiple years. In these situations, the number of years is determined at the beginning of the project.

Identify Intangible Measures

In addition to tangible monetary benefits, most programs derive intangible non-monetary benefits. During data analysis, practitioners make every attempt to convert all data to monetary values. For example, hard data—such as output, quality, and time—are generally always converted to monetary values. Practitioners must also attempt to convert soft data. However, if the conversion process is too subjective or inaccurate, and the resulting values lose credibility in the process, these data are labeled as intangible benefits, and an appropriate explanation is provided. For some programs, intangible benefits have extreme value, often commanding as much attention and influence as the hard data items (Moseley and Larson, 1994). Intangible benefits include such items as the following:

- Improved public image

- Increased job satisfaction

- Increased organizational commitment

- Enhanced technology leadership

- Reduced stress

- Improved teamwork

- Improved customer service

This is not to say that these measures cannot be converted to money; rather, these are measures that typically do not need to be converted to money, as they stand on their own quite well. In addition, to convert some measures to monetary values requires more resources than the entire evaluation, and the results are sometimes still not perceived as credible. A general rule of thumb when it comes to data conversion is:

When in doubt, leave it out.

It is better to have a lower ROI with strong intangibles than to inflate the ROI by spending more on analysis and risking credibility. Figure 4 provides a four-part test to determine whether or not you should convert a measure to money.

Figure 4. To Convert or Not to Convert

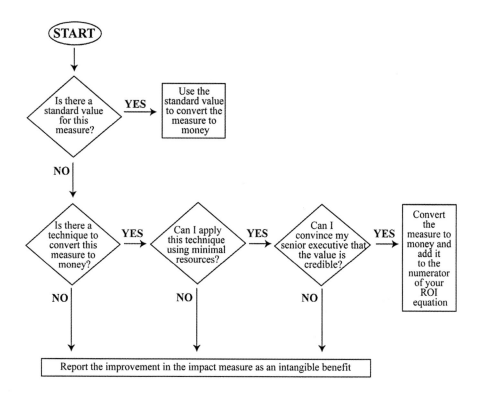

By following the steps in the ROI Methodology, six types of data evolve. Together, these data generate the chain of impact that occurs as organizations invest in their people, as shown in Figure 5. This chain of impact occurs when participants engage in a program; when they react to the program; when they acquire the requisite knowledge, skill, and information; and when they apply that knowledge, skill, and information to the job or project. As a consequence of their application, key business measures improve. We know that this improvement is due to the program, because the effects of the program are isolated from other influences. Impact measures are then converted to money and compared to the cost to generate the ROI. In addition, intangible benefits are reported. These six types of data tell the complete story of program success.

Figure 5. Chain of Impact

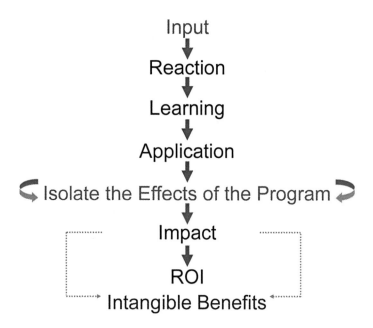

Reporting

The final stage in the ROI Methodology addresses the communication of results. This critical step includes several issues that are often neglected in the evaluation process. The communication process is often just as important as the evaluation itself, and what information is reported and how the information is reported are important concerns.

There are five key reasons why communicating results effectively is so important.

1. **Measurement and evaluation mean nothing without communication.** When an organization communicates the findings of a measurement and evaluation process to the appropriate audience at the appropriate time and in an effective manner, it creates a full loop from the program results to necessary actions based on those results.

2. **Communicating results is necessary to make improvements.** During program evaluation, information is collected at different points in time. Providing feedback to the various groups at each step along the way will allow for adjustments and provide opportunities for improvement. Even after the program is complete, communication is necessary to make sure that the target audience understands the results achieved and how the results can enhance future programs as well as the current program. Communication is the key to making these important adjustments at all phases of the program.

3. **Communication is necessary to show accountability in programs.** Presenting results that encompass all six types of data will provide evidence of a program's contribution to the organization but can also be quite confusing. Different target audiences need different levels of explanation around results.

4. **Communication is a sensitive issue and can be a source of great benefit or a cause of major problems.** Because program results can be closely linked to political issues in an organization, communication can upset some individuals while pleasing others. If certain individuals do not receive the information, or it is delivered inconsistently from one group to another, problems can quickly surface.

5. **A variety of target audiences need different information.** Given that there are so many potential target audiences who require communication about program success, it is important that the communication be tailored directly to their needs. Planning and effort are necessary to make sure that the audience receives all the information it needs in the proper format and at the proper time. The scope of analysis along with the make up and size of the audience are key considerations. Communicating results effectively is essential to the success of the ROI Methodology. The next chapter provides more detail around this topic.

CHAPTER 4: COMMUNICATING RESULTS

Communicating results is the last step in the ROI Methodology. It is an important issue, and one that deserves some attention. Communicating the results of a comprehensive measurement and evaluation process should be systematic and carefully planned.

This chapter describes the last stage in the ROI Methodology. It begins with a brief case study, describes a communication model, and ends with a look at reporting results at a macro level.

The Case of Joan Kravitz

Joan Kravitz had faced the executive team several times in the past, but today was different. Senior executives were keenly interested in the results of her project. With what she knew about the results and her approach in evaluating the program, she felt confident. Even so, her nerves were slightly on edge.

Joan's project was an ROI study on the company's leadership development program facilitated by a prestigious business school. Holding that certificate was not only a display of capability but a badge of honor for many. The program was expensive and had been conducted for leaders in the company for five years. Although the executives supported the program, pushing it to record levels of funding, the top executives offered Joan a challenge—they wanted to know if the program was adding real value to the organization. They wanted to see the ROI.

As Joan scanned the audience, she knew the perspectives of the different audience members. The CEO was not there today, but the rest of the senior team was present. She was disappointed, because the CEO was the champion of her project. However, an urgent schedule change prohibited him from being there, so she had to schedule a private session with him later to cover the agenda. The CFO seemed to support the program, but he was concerned about budgets, costs, and the value of every project, including this project. The operations vice president (VP) saw the program as helpful but was still concerned about business value. The VP of design and engineering did not support the program and rarely nominated participants for it. The VP of marketing was a solid supporter of the program. The executive VP of HR was a very strong supporter of the program and was actively involved in various parts of it. The remaining members of the group were largely neutral, but they were interested in the outcome of her study.

Joan had 30 minutes to demonstrate results and secure approval for her proposed changes to the program that were made evident by the study. As part of the presentation, she planned to walk them through her evaluation approach to ensure they viewed her results as solid. She was actually a little fearful that they might like her analysis so much that they would want to use it for all programs. Her mind was racing with all the "what ifs" that are typical before presenting to key decision makers.

The Presentation

"Good morning, colleagues," Joan began. "Thank you for coming to see the value of a program that you have supported for several years. Is there anyone in the room not familiar with the Advanced Leadership Program?" No one raised a hand. "Well, then, as you know, this program has enjoyed a five-year history with our company, and it has involved over 200 participants. Today, we are going to share the results of a study conducted with the cohort from last year. While these results are intriguing and impressive, they do point to some important changes we need to make, and I want to secure your approval for these changes."

So far, so good, Joan thought to herself. She began to get comfortable as she described a program for which she felt great passion and an evaluation process that she believed provided the most credible and meaningful output of those she researched.

"Our method of choice to evaluate this program is the ROI Methodology, adopted by 5,000 organizations," she said. "It is the most-used evaluation system in the world, and it is ideal for measuring this type of program, because it captures more than ROI. It captures reaction to the program, learning about the program content, application of the content, business impact, and intangibles. It operates with a system of logical processes and uses conservative standards that you will find to be very credible and convincing.

There are two issues to bear in mind. First, the entire cost of the program was used in the ROI calculation, including the executive time away from work. Second, for individual projects, we claimed only one year of monetary value on the benefit side, to keep the benefits conservative and realistic. However, for the team projects that are currently being implemented throughout the organization, a three-year payoff was used, which is still conservative. These assumptions were endorsed by finance and accounting. They are also reflected in Guiding Principles 9 and 10 on the list of 12 Guiding Principles in front of you. These standards shaped our assumptions throughout the implementation of the model, resulting in greater reliability in the data than had we failed to follow them. As you are about to see, the results of this study are categorized using the framework shown here."

She showed the five-level framework. "The framework provides a logical flow of results, beginning with the investment (Level 0) all the way through to ROI (Level 5) and the intangible benefits. It is important to note that all levels of data are important in framing our decision to make the changes I will propose shortly. For now, here are the results."

Reaction and Learning
"The first two levels of results, reaction and learning, are presented first. While these may not be of much interest to you, we knew that the project could go astray if the participants didn't see value in them. Also, if they didn't really learn anything about themselves, their team, or their own competencies, then there wouldn't be any subsequent actions,

behavior change, or impact. Fortunately, we have very positive reaction and learning results."

Joan took two minutes to cover Level 1 (Reaction) and Level 2 (Learning), and then she quickly moved into Level 3 (Application).

Application

"Application data describe the extent to which these executives are changing the way they work, changing their behavior from a leadership perspective," Joan continued. She spent three minutes describing the table with the application data. "At this point, it is appropriate to examine the barriers and enablers—the important issues that inhibit or enhance application. Here are the barriers for these executives to use this program. As you can see, they are not very strong, but it is good to know what they are. If this program had significant barriers, we would want to work on them quickly."

Joan had now been speaking for 10 minutes and would focus on impact and ROI for the remainder of the presentation. Up to this point, to her surprise, there were no questions.

Business Impact

"In terms of business impact, we examined three sets of data," Joan explained. "The first was the individual projects that the participants took on, centered on an important business measure in their particular unit. They demonstrated improvements to these measures using action plans. Your report includes a copy of an action plan and sample copies of completed ones. This chart shows a sampling of individual projects, highlighting the specific measures selected and the amount of money the improvements represent, because participants actually converted the improvements to money. These improvements, which were monitored six months after the action plans were initiated, were impressive. The chart also shows the basis for this conversion and addresses another important issue: isolating the effects of this program." Joan suddenly felt anxious.

"As you know, when any improvement is made, there are multiple factors that can drive it," she continued. "The executives selected measures that are often influenced by various factors, and sometimes we implement programs that are aimed at those improvements. As a result, we must sort out the impact of this program from other influences. The best method for accomplishing this is comparing an experimental group against a control group, where one group of executives is involved in this program and another is not. As you can imagine, this won't work here, because they all have different measures from different business units. Instead, we relied on the executives to provide this information. These data are still credible, because they are coming from the individuals who have achieved the results. We see no reason why they would overstate results attributable to this program.

"This information was collected in a very nonthreatening, unbiased way," continued Joan. "We asked each executive to list any other factors that could have contributed to the improvement in the business measures. They then provided the percent of improvement that should be attributed to this program. To adjust for error in the estimate, we asked them another question: 'What is your confidence on the allocation you just provided, on a scale of 0 to 100 percent?' This served as our error adjustment. For example, if someone was 80 percent confident on an allocation to the program, that reflects 20 percent error, so we would remove the 20 percent. This is achieved by multiplying the 80 percent. Let me take you through an example."

Joan described one particular participant and followed the data through the chart to show the value. In the example, an executive had reported an improvement with three other factors causing it. He allocated 25 percent to the leadership program and was 70 percent confident with that. In that case, 17.5 percent (25 percent x 70 percent) was allocated to the program.

As expected, this table attracted a lot of interest and many questions. Joan spent a few minutes responding to those in a very confident manner.

The CFO asked, "If I want to see this particular measure," pointing to a particular individual, "I could go to that business unit and find the measure and track what has changed."

"Yes," responded Joan. "You can see the actual unit value of that measure, and we can provide the business unit if you would like. We did not use specific names on the chart, because we did not want this to appear to be performance evaluation. This is a process-improvement initiative; if the program doesn't work, we need to adjust it and not necessarily go after the participant. So, we can provide the business units if you want to do that kind of audit."

"There is really no need to do that; I was just curious," responded the CFO.

"Please remember that the groups took on a team project and that this particular group of people had four projects," Joan continued. "Three of those projects have been implemented, and the fourth is still underway. So we did not count any value for the fourth project. For the three projects implemented, we used a three-year payoff. These projects represented needed changes in the organization. Let me quickly describe the three projects."

Joan methodically described these projects, showing their monetary value, the assumptions that were made, and the isolation issue. This took about five minutes, but attracted interest, and she fielded more questions from the executives.

Joan presented a summary of the monetary values from individual and team projects to show the money saved or generated because of the leadership program. She reminded the audience that the amount claimed was connected to the leadership program, isolated from other influences.

Next, she presented the cost. Joan had previously reviewed the cost categories with finance and accounting, and they agreed with her. In fact, Brenda, her finance and accounting representative, had joined her at the meeting. After showing the detailed cost table, with a quick cost summary discussion, Joan noted that all costs were included. She turned to Brenda and asked for her assessment of the categories of cost that were listed. Brenda confirmed that all costs seemed to be covered, and some items were included that might not be necessary. For example, the time away from work probably should not be included, because these executives got their jobs done regardless. Joan added, "We wanted to be consistent and credible, so we have included all costs." She quickly looked at the CFO and could see that he was really intrigued and pleased with this part of the presentation.

ROI

Finally, Joan showed the ROI calculation, presented in two ways. The first ROI assessment, based on individual projects alone, generated an ROI of 48 percent.

"We have a standard that, if someone does not provide you with data, then you assume it had no value," said Joan. "Of the 30 people in this session, six did not provide data, perhaps for good reason. Because the data were not there, we included zero for them. This is Guiding Principle 6."

"When the team projects are included, the number is staggering: 831 percent ROI," she continued. "Please remember, the data on these projects have been approved by the executives involved in the program. Only the portion of the project that is connected directly to the program is used in the calculation, recognizing that other factors could have influenced these particular data sets. So this is a huge value add from the program."

Intangibles

Joan then moved on to the intangibles. She had asked the participants the extent to which this program was influencing certain measures that were largely intangible; key measures were listed in a chart in the report. This also attracted some interest from the executives, as Joan described how the table was constructed. The CFO asked about connecting these measures to monetary values.

"They have not been converted to money in our organization," Joan replied, "but some organizations have done so, and we recommend that we pursue more of those types of conversions. The current trend is to convert more of the classic intangibles to money. This would be a good time to focus on this task."

The CFO agreed.

Conclusion and Recommendations

Joan quickly concluded with a summary and recommendations based on comments from participants. The team project seemed to be a bit cumbersome and generated a lot of frustration with the participants. They suggested that the individual project should be enough. They pointed out that, since this program had been operating for some time, many of the really challenging and necessary projects had already been addressed. While new ones could be generated, it could be an optional part of the process.

Joan recommended to the group that the team project become optional.

However, after some discussion, the executives concluded that the projects should remain part of the process, with administrative support provided to help the executives in the future. Joan added that some support had always been provided and was accounted for in the project cost, but having more support available would certainly be helpful.

This decision underscored the support for the program and the results that Joan had presented. She concluded the conversation by asking if there were any other major programs that should be evaluated at this level, but she cautioned that this level of evaluation takes resources for the team to conduct the study as well as the cost of having it reviewed by an external expert. The executives identified two other projects they wanted to see evaluated at this level.

The CFO said that it was a good presentation and that he appreciated the effort. Joan was pleased, and the HR executive was elated. "This was exactly what we need to be doing, Joan," she said. "You have done an amazing job."

Joan felt good about her work. Conducting the evaluation was a major project, but the insights it provided were invaluable. The program was working, and she made that evident in her presentation. Even though her proposed change to the program was denied, it was clear that the senior team valued the Advanced Leadership Program as originally designed and accepted her approach to demonstrating its value as credible.

Communication Process Model

As demonstrated in Joan's case study, communicating results can be unnerving. This effort, like program evaluation, should be viewed as a process. Figure 6 provides a model of the six components necessary to ensure effective communication of program results. It begins like any project—analyzing the real need for the communication.

Figure 6. Communication Process Model

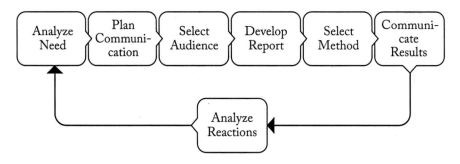

Analyze Need

The first step in the communication model is to analyze the need for the communication. There are many reasons why it is important to communicate the results of a program, including:

- To secure approval for programs
- To gain support for the various functions
- To obtain commitment from participants in programs

- To build credibility for programs
- To reinforce the processes necessary to implement programs
- To explain the various issues around particular programs
- To demonstrate the importance of measuring results
- To market new and existing programs
- To satisfy clients' concerns regarding investments in various programs

Each individual organization should review its specific reasons and tailor its communication strategy around its needs.

Plan the Communication

Just as planning the evaluation process is important, so is planning the communication process. Thorough planning will ensure that the communication addresses both client concerns and issues important to the program staff and the general audience. Three issues are important in planning the communication of results:

1. Communication guidelines
2. Communication about specific programs
3. Communication of the ROI impact study

Communication Guidelines

When examining the complete program or project implementation process, there should be guidelines for how the results will be communicated. These issues range from providing feedback during program implementation to communicating the ROI from an impact study. Seven areas should be considered in developing communication:

1. What will actually be communicated?
It is important to detail the types of information communicated throughout the program.

2. **When will the data be communicated?**
   As with most projects and processes, timing is critical in communicating results.

3. **How will the information be communicated?**
   This shows preferences toward particular types of communication media. For example, some organizations prefer to have written documents, while others prefer face-to-face meetings, and still others prefer electronic forms of communication.

4. **Where will the communication take place?**
   For some audiences, it may be more appropriate to present data in a formal on-site meeting; for others, it may be more appropriate to present data at an off-site, less formal location. The location is important in terms of convenience and perception.

5. **Who will communicate the results?**
   Who the messenger will be is another important issue to consider when developing the overall communication strategy. Is it most appropriate for the program manager to present results? An independent third party?

6. **Who should receive the information?**
   Identifying the target audience is another crucial issue. The client should receive a detailed report or, at the least, a presentation that reflects the detailed information. The general population of the organization should receive highlights. Ensuring that the appropriate audience receives the appropriate information is critical in achieving the desired response.

7. **What actions are required or desired as a result of the communication?**
   The final consideration in developing the communication plan is determining what actions are required or desired as a result of the communication. A communication to the program staff may explain changes that need to be made to the program; a communi-

cation to senior executives may be a call for a change in priorities. Clearly stating the desired outcomes of the communication is an important part of developing the overall strategy.

Communication About Specific Programs

Communication planning should occur at the same time as evaluation planning for a specific program or project. The communication plan document is an output of this planning process. This plan details how specific information will be developed and shared with various groups and what actions will be expected. In addition, this plan details how the overall results will be communicated, the time frames for communication, and the appropriate groups to receive information.

Communication of the ROI Impact Study

The final issue regarding communication planning is the communication of the final ROI impact study. The presentation of this study occurs at the completion of the evaluation process, when the results of all levels of evaluation have been analyzed. Different audiences need different levels of detail. For instance, the evaluation team and program staff will generally always receive a copy of the complete report. This complete report details the need for and objectives of the program as well as the methodology used and the results of the evaluation. The data collection instruments and raw data appear in an appendix.

When the evaluation process becomes routine, and senior and executive management are familiar with the process and the reporting format, a one-page summary of results can be used. This one-page report provides the essential details and program results in a brief, bottomline format. A sample of this scorecard is available for downloading at www.thebottomlineonroi.com. A word of caution: while this report provides a simple look at the results, it is not advisable to begin reporting results in this format until the evaluation process is well supported within an organization and by senior and executive management. Also, as will be explained later, a formal presentation should be made to senior staff at least once to ensure that they understand the process and perceive the results as credible.

Communication to other audiences may come in the form of general interest overviews, general interest articles, and marketing materials. Some of these will be discussed in more detail later. Table 16 is a sample communication plan, in which a complete report is provided for the client, staff, and project team. A much briefer report is provided for senior management. A general report is provided to participants. This step not only provides participants with program results but also builds the credibility of the ROI Methodology. Participants spend time completing questionnaires and participating in focus groups and interviews during the evaluation process. As part of their participation, they should be provided with the results.

A general interest article can be printed in a company publication. This type of article keeps accountability for the learning and development, performance improvement, and/or HR functions in front of the employees at large. Finally, ROI results are published in marketing brochures to recruit participants for future programs. The key is to plan the communication of the final impact study with the various report types and audiences in mind.

Table 16. Communication Plan

COMMUNICATION PLAN

Impact-Study Report	Target Audience	Distribution Method
Complete report (100 pages)	Client team Staff Project team	Special meeting
Executive summary (8 pages)	Senior management	Routine meeting
General interest overview and summary (10 pages)	Participants	Mail with letter
General interest article (1 page)	All employees	Company newsletter
Brochure highlighting project objectives and specific results	Team leaders Other clients	Marketing materials

Select the Audience

To the greatest extent possible, the target audience for any communication should be identified in advance. Understanding audience needs and issues will ensure that the appropriate data from the evaluation process are communicated and that the desired results of the communication are achieved.

Along with understanding client needs and issues, there should also be a clear understanding of audience bias. While many audience members will quickly support the program results, others will be skeptical or even resentful. Understanding and expecting these preconceived biases will assist in ensuring that the communication process mitigates them. Some key questions to ask when assessing the audience are the following:

- Are they interested in the program?

- Do they want to receive the information?

- Has someone already made a commitment to them regarding communication?

- Is the timing right for this audience?

- Are they familiar with the program?

- How do they prefer to have results communicated?

- Are they likely to find the results threatening?

- Which medium will be most convincing to them?

Develop the Report

The next step in the communication process is to develop the final product—the comprehensive ROI evaluation impact-study report. This report presents the complete results of the ROI Methodology. As mentioned previously, the impact study provides details of the evaluation along with supporting documents and summary results. A basic report is usually divided into three sections: background information, results, and conclusions and recommendations.

Background Information

Background information describes the need for and scope of the program. It includes the objectives and information on content, duration, course materials, facilitators, location, and other specific items.

Methodology

Describing the methodology before the results puts the results into context. This section assures the audience that results are credible and reliable to the extent possible under the study's limitations and delimitations. The description is detailed enough that the audience will understand the evaluation approach and how they would go about replicating the study if there were an opportunity to do so. Along with information on the process, this section of the study includes data collection and data analysis strategies, instrumentation, sources of data, timing of data collection, isolation and data conversion techniques used, and cost categories considered.

Results

The next section presents the results of the evaluation. Each type of data generated by the ROI Methodology is reported, beginning with Level 0 (Input), representing the program activity, then on to results at Level 1 (Reaction), and ending with intangible benefits. This balanced set of measures tells the entire story of program success. While ROI is a critical measure in the reporting process, it is only one of six measures of results. By presenting the results in order of the chain of impact, the audience better understands the connection between the program and the ROI.

Conclusions and Recommendations

This section of the impact-study report presents the conclusions and brief explanations of how each conclusion came about. The section also includes a list of recommendations for changes to the program, with brief explanations. It is important that the conclusions and recommendations be consistent with one another and with the findings described in the previous section.

Table 17 provides a sample table of contents from an ROI study, representing these four major sections. A complete impact study can vary in length from 20 to 30 pages for a small project up to 200 or more pages for a comprehensive evaluation. Remember that not all audiences need this detailed information. The key is to analyze the target audiences and develop reports that answer their questions in such a way that they view the results as credible and meaningful.

Table 17. ROI Study Outline

Sample Table of Contents for an ROI Impact Study

Table of Contents
List of Tables
List of Figures
List of Exhibits

Part I The Challenge
    Section 1: Introduction
    Section 2: Program Description

Part II The Methodology
    Section 3: Model for Impact Study
    Section 4: Data Collection Strategy
    Section 5: Data Analysis Strategy

Part III The Results
    Section 6: Input
    Section 7: Reaction and Planned Action
    Section 8: Learning
    Section 9: Application and Implementation
          — Enablers to Application
          — Barriers to Application
    Section 10: Business Impact
    Section 11: ROI and Its Meaning
          — Monetary Benefits
          — Program Costs
          — ROI Calculation
    Section 12: Intangible Benefits

Part IV Recommendations

Section 13: Conclusions and Recommendations
Section 14: Suggestions for Improvement

Part V Appendix

Select the Method

There are many options available for communicating results. In addition to the actual report, the most frequently used methods are management meetings, interim and progress reports, organization publications, and case studies.

Management Meetings

Management meetings are fertile ground for the communication of program results. All organizations have a variety of meetings and, in the proper context, program results can be an important part of each kind of meeting. Management meetings include staff meetings, supervisory meetings, panel discussions, and management association meetings.

Interim and Progress Reports

Interim and progress reports are brief reports mailed or emailed to the appropriate target audiences. A progress report can be something as simple as a "flash report" that appears when employees log on to email; employees have the option to read it when they log on initially or to save it for later.

Organization Publications

Many organizations have newsletters or quarterly publications that keep employees abreast of the latest news and issues. Including program results in these publications can serve a number of purposes, including arousing general interest. A safety program may be evaluated to determine its impact on lost-time accidents. When the evaluation finds that the program does indeed impact lost-time accidents, an article can highlight these results. Stories about participants involved in a program and the results they achieve may help to generate interest in a program on the part of employees who would not otherwise have known about it. Reports of program success in organization publications can bring recognition to participants in the program. This public recognition can help to build confidence and self-esteem in the individuals highlighted.

Case Studies

The use of case studies is an effective way to communicate the results of a program evaluation. It is recommended that a few projects be developed in a case-study format. A typical case study describes the situation; provides appropriate background information, including the events that led to the program; presents the techniques and strategies used to develop the study; and highlights the key issues in the program and the evaluation.

Case studies can be used in group discussions, allowing interested individuals to react to the material, offer different perspectives, and draw conclusions about approaches or techniques. They can serve as self-teaching guides as individuals try to understand how evaluation is developed and used in the organization. They can also provide appropriate recognition for those who were involved in the actual case study or achieved the results.

The important issue is to understand which method is most effective for the target audience and to include that decision in the overall communication strategy.

Communicate Results

The next step is the actual presentation of results. There are generally two issues to consider:

- Providing feedback

- Presenting results to senior management

Providing Feedback

The first issue is the feedback provided throughout the program being evaluated. This information is communicated primarily to the staff and project team. Feedback data provide information that suggests what immediate changes are necessary for continuous improvement.

Presenting Results to Senior Management

The second issue to consider concerns communication to senior management. Two questions that should be asked when planning communication to this group are "Do they believe you?" and "Can they take it?" If these two concerns are addressed at the outset, they are not as big an issue when it is time to present the final results.

In responding to the first question, "Do they believe you?" the key is to ensure that, when a program reaps a very high ROI, the presentation of the results includes all the steps covered in Table 18 on page 91. Beginning with background information on the program and a description of the ROI Methodology will build credibility in the results and the evaluation process. Ensuring that the audience understands that efforts were made to be conservative in the evaluation will also build credibility. In addition, reporting results in order and including each level will show senior management all the elements that go into the ROI evaluation. If the ROI is presented up front, there is a risk that the audience will not hear the rest of the presentation. Their focus will be on the end results, not on the process.

The second question, "Can they take it?" refers to the fact that, occasionally, a program may result in a less-than-desirable or even negative ROI. While no one wants a negative ROI, the ROI Methodology is not an individual performance evaluation—it is a process-improvement tool. Negative ROIs can be invaluable sources of information on necessary changes and improvements—not only for the program being evaluated but for systems and processes supporting program implementation. In communicating low or negative ROIs, follow the same outline provided in Table 18. However, there should also be a plan for addressing the issues causing the negative ROI. If the program was too expensive, then acknowledge this and disclose a plan to reduce costs in the future. If the program was inappropriate for the problem being addressed, the needs assessment process may need to be adjusted. If there were barriers to implementing the skills learned and/or knowledge acquired during the program, identify those barriers and present them along with a solution for their removal. If the program proves to have been just plain ineffective, kill it and move on to something more useful to employees and the organization. The important point is to view low and negative ROIs as opportunities to make positive changes. When presenting these types of ROIs, be sure to present plans for improvement or next steps.

Analyze Reactions

The final step in the communication process is analyzing reactions to the communication. As with any process, evaluation of the communication is critical to understanding where improvements are necessary. Communication is important, yet little emphasis is placed on its evaluation. Analyzing reactions to communication will allow for improvements in future reports, presentations, and other communication processes. It will allow for necessary changes in media or timing. It will help to ensure that the key issues for different target audiences are covered and that the results of ROI evaluations are clearly communicated to and understood by future audiences.

During the presentation of results, questions may be asked or the information challenged. This input is important to remember for the next program evaluation. Compiling the questions can be useful in determining what types of information should be included in future communication. Positive comments should also be noted.

Staff meetings are excellent forums for discussing reactions to the presentation of results. Comments can come from many sources, depending on the particular target audiences. When a major presentation on program results is made, a feedback questionnaire may also be used on the entire audience. The purpose of this questionnaire is to determine the extent to which the audience understood and believed the information presented. Another approach to measuring reactions to the presentation of results is to conduct a survey of the management group to determine their perception of training and performance improvement programs.

Macro-Level Reporting

Reporting results of an ROI study answers questions stakeholder ask, such as: "Are our investments in people paying off?" Impact and ROI studies reflect micro-level reporting, meaning they report success at the program level. But, from time to time, someone may ask if the entire function is paying off overall. This is where macro-level reporting comes into play.

Macro-level reporting is a way in which an organization can report on all efforts underway. This takes key measures from micro-level reports and combines them into a macro-level scorecard that reports evaluation activity and results for all programs, up to the level of evaluation at which those programs are evaluated. Table 18 outlines the content of a macro-level scorecard from a large financial institution's corporate university.

Table 18. Outline for Corporate University Scorecard

Corporate University Success

0. Input
1. Number of Employees Involved
2. Total Hours of Involvement
3. Hours Per Employee
4. Training Investment as a Percent of Payroll
5. Cost Per Participant

I. Reaction and Planned Action
1. Percent of Programs Evaluated at this Level
2. Ratings on 7 Items Versus Target
3. Percent with Action Plans
4. Percent with ROI Forecast

II. Learning
1. Percent of Programs Evaluated at this Level
2. Types of Measurements
3. Self-Assessment Ratings on 3 Items Versus Targets
4. Pre-/Post-program—Average Differences

III. Application
1. Percent of Programs Evaluated at this Level
2. Ratings on 3 Items Versus Targets
3. Percent of Action Plans Complete
4. Barriers (List of Top Ten)
5. Enablers (List of Top Ten)
6. Management Support Profile

IV. Business Impact
1. Percentage of Programs Evaluated at this Level
2. Linkage with Measures (List of Top Ten)
3. Types of Measurement Techniques
4. Types of Methods to Isolate the Effects of Programs
5. Investment Perception

V. ROI
1. Percent of Programs Evaluated at this Level
2. ROI Summary for Each Study
3. Methods of Converting Data to Monetary Values
4. Fully Loaded Cost Per Participant

Intangibles
1. List of Intangibles (Top Ten)
2. How Intangibles Were Captured

In addition to creating organization-specific macro-level score-cards, efforts are underway to standardize reporting and align it with other financial reports important to the C-suite. The Center for Talent Reporting, a 501(c)(6) nonprofit organization, is the home for Talent Development Reporting Principles (TDRp), an industry-led grassroots initiative to establish internal reporting principles and standards for human capital. TDRp provides the same type of guidance for HR that Generally Accepted Accounting Principles (GAAP) provides accountants in the US or that International Financial Reporting Standards (IFRS) provides accountants elsewhere. Guidance includes a simple yet comprehensive framework for planning, collecting, defining, and reporting the critical outcome, effectiveness, and efficiency measures that are needed to deliver results and contribute to the success of the organizations. It builds on the framework and model presented in this book, as well as other approaches, in an attempt to help organizations adopt a common vocabulary along with common statements, reports, and processes that will allow everyone involved in the human capital space to have greater impact on the success of their organization. Table 19 is a sample operations report for learning and development. Other sample reports, along with information on their measures library, accreditation process, and implementation guidance, are available on their website at www.centerfortalentreporting.org.

Table 19. Sample TDRp Executive Operations Report

Learning and Development
Sample Executive Operations Report
Results Through June

		2014	2015			
Effectiveness Measures		Actual	Plan	Jun YTD	% Plan	Forecast
Level 1: Participant Feedback (All programs)	% favorable	80%	85%	87%	102%	85%
Level 1: Sponsor Feedback (Select programs)	% favorable	75%	80%	77%	96%	78%
Level 2: Learning (Select programs)	Score	78%	85%	83%	98%	84%
Level 3: Application Rate (Select programs)	% who applied it	61%	75%	78%	104%	79%
Level 4: (Select programs)	% top two boxes	61.0%	75.0%	78.0%	104.0%	78%
Level 5 (Select programs)						
Net benefits	Thousands $	$546	$800	$345	43.1%	$800
ROI	%	29%	35%	32%	91.4%	33%
Efficiency Measures						
Course Management						
Total Developed	Number	22	36	24	67%	35
Number Meeting Deadline	Number	16	33	21	64%	33
% Meeting Deadline	%	73%	92%	88%	95%	94%
Total Delivered	Number	143	178	167	94%	178
Number Meeting Deadline	Number	89	160	139	87%	155
% Meeting Deadline	%	62%	90%	83%	85%	87%
% of courses that are traditional classroom	%	56%	43%	46%	107%	42%
E-learning courses utilization rate	% taken by 20+	83%	97%	91%	94%	97%
% of employees reached by L&D	%	85%	88%	72%		88%
L&D Expenditure	Million $	$15.8	$20.2	$9.9	49%	$20.2
Cost Reduction (Internal to L&D)	Thousand $	$63	$295	$168	57%	$325

Reporting program results is a process. Achieving clarity on the need, planning the communication strategy, selecting the audience, developing the appropriate report, selecting the media, communicating results, and analyzing reactions and taking action accordingly will help ensure evaluation efforts are not in vain.

CHAPTER 5: A SIMPLE CASE STUDY

The fourth piece of the evaluation puzzle introduced in Chapter 2 is case application and practice. This piece of the puzzle represents the practical application of the ROI Methodology. This very simple case study is a classic we use at ROI Institute to demonstrate how the process works. It in no way reflects the vast number or types of programs to which the process can be applied, but it does present the key issues that readers will face as they move forward with application.

The case study describes how a retail store chain evaluated an interactive selling skills program to drive sales in their electronics department. The program was a pilot, and a decision would be made whether or not to launch the full program based on the results. Senior leaders did not want to spend a lot of money on the pilot; therefore, the evaluation investment had to reflect the same resource considerations.

Background Information

Retail Merchandise Company (RMC) is a large national chain of 420 stores, located in most major US markets. RMC sells small household items, gifts of all types, electronics, and jewelry, as well as personal accessories. It does not sell clothes or major appliances. The executives at RMC had been concerned about the slow sales growth and were experimenting with several programs to boost sales. One of the concerns focused on the interaction with customers. Sales associates were not actively involved in the sales process, usually waiting for a customer to make a purchasing decision and then processing the sale. Several store managers had analyzed the situation to determine if more communication with the customer would boost sales. The analysis revealed that the use of very simple techniques to probe and guide the customer to a purchase should indeed boost sales in each store.

The senior executives asked the training and development function to consider a very simple customer interactive skills program for a small group of sales associates. The training staff preferred a program produced by an external supplier to avoid the cost of development, particularly if the program were not effective. The specific charge from the management team was to implement the program in three stores, monitor the results, and make recommendations.

The sales associates were typical of the retail stores' employee profile. They were generally not college graduates, and most had only a few months while some had a few years of retail store experience. Turnover was usually quite high, and formal training had not been a major part of previous sales development efforts.

The Solution

The training and development staff conducted a brief initial needs assessment and identified five simple skills that would need to be covered in the program. From the staff's analysis, it appeared that the sales associates did not have or were very uncomfortable with the use of these skills. The training and development staff selected the "Interactive Selling Skills" program, which made significant use of skill practices. The program was an existing product from an external training supplier that included two days of training, in which participants would have an opportunity to practice each of the skills with a fellow classmate, followed by three weeks of on-the-job application. Then, in a final day of training, there would be discussion of problems, issues, barriers, and concerns with using the skills. Additional practice and fine-tuning of skills would take place in that final one-day session. At RMC, this program was tried in the electronics area of three stores with 16 people trained in each store, for a total of 48 participants. The staff of the training supplier facilitated the program for a predetermined fee.

The Measurement Challenge

The direction from senior management was very clear: these executives wanted to boost sales, and they would determine at the same time if this program represented a financial payoff by offering strategies to implement toward that goal. Business impact and ROI were the measurement mandates from the senior team.

In seeking a process to show ROI, the training and development staff turned to the ROI Methodology. This process generates six types of measures:
- Reaction and Planned Action
- Learning
- Application and Implementation
- Business Impact
- ROI
- Intangible measures

It also includes a technique to isolate the effects of the program or solution.

Figure 7 shows the ROI Methodology process model. Four types of data are collected, representing the four levels of evaluation. The analysis develops a fifth level of data as well as the intangible benefits. The process includes a method to isolate the effects of the program and a method to convert data to monetary value. The fully loaded costs are used to develop the actual ROI. This process was already in place at RMC, and training and development selected it as the method to measure the success of this program.

Figure 7. ROI Methodology Process Model

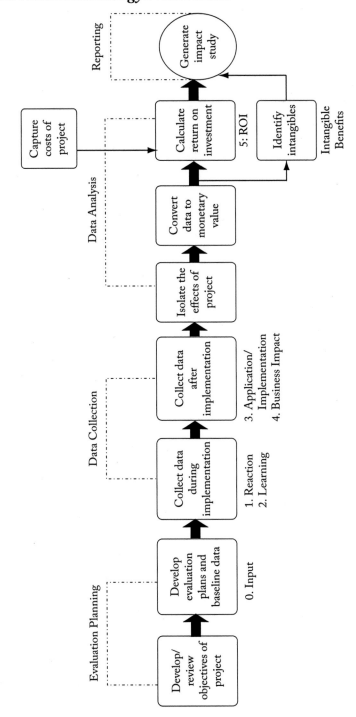

One reason RMC appreciated the model is the standards that support its implementation. These standards, referred to as 12 Guiding Principles, ensure that assumptions made in the analysis are conservative and that the data generated are credible. Table 20 shows the Guiding Principles.

Table 20. Twelve Guiding Principles

GUIDING PRINCIPLES

1. When conducting a higher-level evaluation, collect data at lower levels.

2. When conducting a higher-level evaluation, do not be so comprehensive at the lower levels.

3. When collecting and analyzing data, use only the most credible sources.

4. When analyzing data, select the most conservative alternative for calculations.

5. Use at least one method to isolate the effects of the solution.

6. If no improvement data are available for a population or from a specific source, assume that no improvement has occurred.

7. Adjust estimates of improvement for the potential error in the estimates.

8. Extreme data items and unsupported claims should not be used in ROI calculations.

9. Use only the first year of annual benefits in the ROI analysis of short-term solutions.

10. Fully load costs of the solution when analyzing ROI.

11. Define intangible measures as measures that are purposely not converted to monetary values.

12. Communicate results from the ROI Methodology to all key stakeholders.

Planning for the ROI

An important part of the success of the ROI evaluation is to properly plan for the impact study early in the training and development cycle. Appropriate up-front attention saves time later when data are actually collected and analyzed, thus improving accuracy and reducing the cost of the evaluation. This approach also avoids any confusion surrounding what will be accomplished, by whom, and at what time. Two planning documents are key to the up-front planning, and the training staff completed them before the program was implemented.

Following are descriptions of each document.

Data Collection Plan

Table 21 shows the completed data collection plan for this program. The document provides a space for major elements and issues regarding collecting data for the different levels of evaluation. Broad program objectives are appropriate for planning, as the table shows.

The objective at Level 1 for this program was a positive reaction to the potential use of the skills on the job. The gauge for this level was a reaction questionnaire that participants completed at the end of the program and that facilitators collected. The goal was to achieve four out of five on a composite rating. The questionnaire also asked participants to indicate how often and in which situations they would actually use the skills.

The measurement of learning focused on learning how to use five simple skills. The measure of success was a pass or fail on the skill practice that the facilitator observed and from which he/she collected data on the second day of the program.

For application and implementation evaluation, the objectives focused on two major areas. The first was the initial use of the five simple skills. Success was determined from verbal feedback that the facilitator obtained directly from participants in a follow-up session on the third day of training. The second major objective was for at least 50 percent of the participants to be using all the skills with every customer. This information was obtained on the follow-up questionnaire, scheduled three months after completion of the program, on which the participants rated the frequency of utilization of the skills.

Business impact focused purely on increase in sales. The statistic for average weekly sales per associate was monitored from company records in a three-month follow-up. Finally, a 50 percent ROI target was set, which was much higher than the standard for many other ROI evaluations. Senior executives wanted a significant improvement over the cost of the program to make a decision to move forward with a large-scale implementation.

The data collection plan was an important part of the evaluation strategy. It provided clear direction on the type of data that would be collected, how it would be collected, when it would be collected, and who would collect it.

Table 21. Data Collection Plan

DATA COLLECTION PLAN

Program: _____ Responsibility: _____ Date: _____

Level	Broad Program Objective(s)	Measures	Data Collection Method/Instruments	Data Sources	Timing	Responsibilities
1	**REACTION/SATISFACTION and PLANNED ACTION** • Positive reaction – 4 out of 5 • Action items	• Rating on a composite of five measures • Yes/No	• Questionnaire	• Participant	• End of program (3rd day)	• Facilitator
2	**LEARNING** • Learn to use five simple skills	• Pass/Fail on skill practice	• Observation of skill practice by facilitator	• Facilitator	• 2nd day of program	• Facilitator
3	**APPLICATION/ IMPLEMENTATION** • Initial use of five simple skills • At least 50% of participants use all skills with every customer	• Verbal Feedback • 5th item checked on a 1 to 5 scale	• Follow-up session • Follow-up questionnaire	• Participant • Participant	• 3 weeks after 2nd day • 3 months after program	• Facilitator • Store Training Coordinator
4	**BUSINESS IMPACT** • Increase in Sales	• Weekly average sales per sales associate	• Business performance monitoring	• Company records	• 3 months after program	• Store Training Coordinator
5	**ROI** • 50%	Comments:				

- 101 -

ROI Analysis Plan

Table 22 shows the completed ROI analysis plan, which captures information on several key items necessary to develop the actual ROI calculation. The first column lists the business impact measure. This is in connection with the previous planning document, the data collection plan. The ROI analysis builds from the business impact data by addressing several issues involved in processing the data. The first issue is the method of isolating the effects of the program on that particular business impact measure.

Isolation Techniques

One of the most important parts of this evaluation is isolating the effects of the training program. Selecting the appropriate technique is critical in the planning stage. The key question is: "When sales data are collected three months after the program is implemented, how much of the increase in sales, if any, is directly related to the program?" While the improvement in sales may be linked to the training program, other non-training factors contribute to improvement. The cause-and-effect relationship between training and performance improvement can be very confusing and difficult to prove, but it can be accomplished with an acceptable degree of accuracy. In the planning process, the challenge is to develop one or more specific strategies to isolate the effects of training and include at least one of these in the ROI analysis plan.

In this case study, the issue was relatively easy to address. Senior executives gave the training and development staff the freedom to select any stores for implementation of the pilot program. The performance of the three stores selected for the program was compared with the performance of three other stores that were identical in every way possible. This control group analysis approach represents the most accurate way to isolate the effects of a program. Fortunately, other strategies from the list of 10 approaches in the ROI process, such as trend line analysis and estimation, would also be feasible. Control group analysis was selected as the best method for the situation.

The challenge in the control group arrangement was to appropriately select both sets of stores. The control group of three stores would not receive the training, whereas the pilot group would. It was important for those stores to be as identical as possible, so the training and development staff developed several criteria that could influence sales. This list became quite extensive and included market data, store-level data, management and leadership data, and individual differences. In a conference call with regional managers, the list was pared down to the four most likely influences. The executives selected those influences that would count for at least 80 percent of the differences in weekly store sales per associate. These criteria were as follows:

- *Store size,* where the larger stores commanded a higher performance level

- *Store location,* defined by a market variable of median household income in the area where customers live

- *Customer traffic levels,* which measures the flow of traffic through the store; this measure, originally developed for security purposes, provides an excellent indication of customer flow through the store

- *Previous store performance,* a good predictor of future performance; the training and development staff collected six months of data for weekly sales per associate to identify the two groups

As a fallback position, in case the control group arrangement did not work, participant estimates were planned. In this approach, the individuals would be provided with their performance data and would be asked to indicate the extent to which the training program influenced their contribution. This data would be adjusted for the error of the estimate and used in the analysis.

Data Conversion Techniques

The team knew they would have to convert business impact measures to money to calculate the ROI. Given that their key measure was sales, this part of the process was relatively easy. While sales are important to the company, it is the profit on the sales that is the value add.

So, as shown in the third column on Table 22, they used the standard profit contribution for the store.

Cost Categories

The next column focuses on the key cost categories that would be included in the fully loaded cost profile. There were no real needs assessment costs in this case, and it was an off-the-shelf program, so development costs were included in the fee paid for facilitation and program materials. Other costs as shown in the table were meals, facilities, participants' time in the program, and coordination and evaluation. The team agreed that these represented all costs associated with the program.

Intangible Benefits

Intangible benefits are those benefits not converted to money. Two intangible measures that were important to the organization were customer satisfaction and employee satisfaction. The team added those to the planning document to keep an eye on potential improvements resulting from the program.

Communication Targets

While a separate communication plan would be developed, it was important during the evaluation planning process to identify the specific audiences to whom the report would be delivered. As shown on the table, there were several audiences with which these results would be shared.

Other Influences

Finally, the last column listed any particular influences or issues that might have an effect on the implementation. The training staff identified three issues, with two being very critical to the evaluation. No communication was planned with the control group, so there would be no potential for contamination from the pilot group. In addition, because seasonal fluctuation could affect the control group arrangement, this evaluation was positioned between Father's Day and the winter holiday season, thereby eliminating the variable of the huge surges in volume during those times.

Table 22. ROI Analysis Plan

ROI ANALYSIS PLAN

Program: _____   Responsibility: _____   Date: _____

Data Items	Methods of Isolating the Effects of the Program	Methods of Converting Data	Cost Categories	Intangible Benefits	Communication Targets	Other Influences/Issues
• Weekly Sales Per Associate	• Control Group Analysis • Participant Estimate	• Standard Value: Profit Contribution	• Facilitation Fees • Program Materials • Meals/ Refreshments • Facilities • Participant Salaries/Benefits • Cost of Coordination/ Evaluation	• Customer Satisfaction • Employee Satisfaction	• Program Participants • Electronics Dept. Managers – Target Stores • Store Managers – Target Stores • Senior Store Executives District, Region, Headquarters • Training Staff: Instructors, Coordinators, Designers, and Managers	• Must Have Job Coverage During Training • No Communication with Control Group • Seasonal Fluctuations Should Be Avoided

The data collection plan together with the ROI analysis plan provided detailed information on calculating the ROI and illustrated how the process would develop and be analyzed. When completed, these two planning documents provided the direction necessary for the ROI evaluation.

Results

The pilot program proved to be successful for the three stores participating. The results are shown below.

Reaction and Learning

The first two levels of evaluation, reaction and learning, were simple and straightforward. The training staff collected five measures of reaction to determine if the objectives had been met. The overall objective was to obtain at least four out of five on a composite of these five measures. As Table 23 illustrates, the overall objective was met. Of the specific measures, the relevance of the material and the usefulness of the program were considered to be the two most important. In addition, 90 percent of the participants had action items indicating when and how often they would use these skills. Collectively, this Level 1 data gave assurance that sales associates had a very favorable reaction to the program.

The measurement of learning was accomplished with simple skill practice sessions observed by the facilitator. Each associate practiced each of the five skills, and the facilitator inserted a check mark on the questionnaire when the associate was successful. While this approach was subjective, it was felt that it provided enough evidence that the participants had actually learned these basic skills.

Table 23. Level 1 Reaction Data on Selected Data

Success with Objectives	4.3
Relevance of Material	4.4
Usefulness of Program	4.5
Exercises/Skill Practices	3.9
Overall Instructor Rating	4.1
Composite Score	4.2
Target Score	4.0

Application and Implementation

To measure application and implementation, the training and development staff administered a follow-up questionnaire three months after the end of the program. The questionnaire was comprehensive, spanning 20 questions on three pages, and was collected anonymously to reduce the potential for bias from participants. The questionnaire covered the following topics:

• Action plan implementation

• Relevance of the program

• Use of skills

• Changes in work routine

• Linkage with department measures

• Other benefits

• Barriers

• Enablers

• Management support

• Suggestions for improvement

• Other comments

While all the information was helpful, the information on the use of skills was most critical. Table 24 shows the results from two of the 20 questions on the questionnaire. The first one provided some assurance that the participants were using the skills, as 78 percent strongly agreed that they apply the skills. More important, the next question focused directly on one of the goals of the program. Fifty-two percent indicated that they use the skills with each customer, slightly exceeding the goal of 50 percent.

Table 24. Level 3 Selected Application Data on Two of 20 Questions

	Strongly Agree	Agree	Neither Agree nor Disagree	Disagree	Strongly Disagree
I utilize the skills taught in the program.	78%	22%	0%	0%	0%
	With Each Customer	Every Third Customer	Several Times Each Day	At Least Once Daily	At Least Once Weekly
Frequency of use of skills	52%	26%	19%	4%	0%

Because these are simple skills, with the opportunity to use them every day, the follow-up session three weeks after the first two days of training provided the first, early indication of skill transfer to the job. If the skills were still being used three months after training, it would be safe to conclude that the majority of the participants had internalized them.

It is important to understand the rationale for using the questionnaire rather than one of the many other data collection methods. The most accurate method would be observation of the participants on the job by a third party. In that scenario, the "mystery shoppers" must learn the skills and be allowed to rate each of the 48 participants. This approach would provide concrete evidence that the participants had transferred the skills. This approach would be expensive, and it would not be necessary under the circumstances. Because the management team was more interested in business impact and ROI, it had less interest in the lower levels of evaluation. Although some data should be collected to have assurance that the skills have transferred, the process does not have to be so comprehensive. Guiding Principle 2 of the ROI Methodology comes into play with this issue. When an evaluation is undertaken at a higher level, an earlier and lower-level evaluation does not have to be comprehensive. This does not mean that Level 3 data cannot or should not be collected. With limited resources, shortcuts must be developed, and this principle allows us to use a less expensive approach. If the management team had asked for more evidence of customer interaction or wanted to know the quality and thoroughness of the actual exchange of information, then a more comprehensive Level 3 evaluation would be required, and perhaps the evaluation would even have stopped at Level 3.

Business Impact

Weekly sales data were collected for three months after the program for both groups. Table 25 shows the data for the first three weeks after training, along with the last three weeks during the evaluation period. An average for the last three weeks is more appropriate than data for a single week, because any single week could have a spike effect that could affect the results. As the data show, there was a significant difference between the two groups, indicating that the training program was improving sales. The percent increase that was directly attributable to the sales training was approximately 15 percent. If a business impact evaluation were all that was required, this data would provide the information needed to show that the program has improved sales. However, if the ROI is needed, two more steps are necessary.

Table 25. Level 4 Data on Average Weekly Sales

Weeks After Training	Trained Group ($)	Control Group ($)
1	$9,723	$9,698
2	9,978	9,720
3	10,424	9,812
13	13,690	11,572
14	11,491	9,683
15	11,044	10,092
Average for Weeks 13, 14, 15	$12,075	$10,449

Converting Data to a Monetary Value

To convert the business data to a monetary value, the training and development staff had to address several issues. First, it was necessary to convert the actual sales differences to value-added data—in this case, profits. The store-level profit margin of 2 percent was multiplied by the difference or increase in sales. Table 26 shows the calculation, as the weekly sales per associate of $1,626 became a value-added amount of $32.50. Because 46 participants were still on the job in three months, the value-added amount was multiplied by 46, for a weekly total of $1,495.

The mention of those 46 participants also evokes Guiding Principle 6. That principle says, "If no improvement data are available for a population or from a specific source, it is assumed that little or no improvement has occurred." This is a conservative approach, because the missing data are assumed to have no value. Two of the participants were no longer on the job, and this rule was used to exclude any contribution from that group instead of tracking what happened to them. However, the cost to train them would be included, although their values were not part of the contribution calculation.

Finally, annual benefits were used to develop a total benefit for the program. The ROI concept is an annual value, and only the first-year benefits are used for short-term training programs. This is Guiding Principle 9. Although this approach may slightly overstate the benefits for the first year, it is considered conservative, because it does not capture any improvements or benefits in the second, third, or future years. In summary, the total annualized program benefit was $71,760.

Table 26. Annualized Program Benefits for 46 Participants

Average weekly sales per employee trained group	$12,075
Average weekly sales per employee untrained group	10,449
Increase	1,626
Profit contribution (2% of stores sales)	32.50
Total weekly improvement (x 46)	1,495
Total Annual Benefits (x 48 weeks)	**$71,760**

Program Cost

The program costs, shown in Table 27, are fully loaded and represent all the major categories outlined earlier. This is a conservative approach, as described in Guiding Principle 10. In this case, the costs for the development were included in the facilitation fee, since the external supplier produced the program. As for the cost of the participants, time away from the job is the largest of the cost items, and this can be included, or the lost opportunity can be included, but not both. To be consistent, this is usually developed as the total time away from work (three days) multiplied by the daily compensation rate including a 35 percent benefits factor. Finally, the estimated cost for the evaluation and the coordination of data collection was included. Since the company had an internal evaluation staff certified in the ROI process, the overall cost for this project was quite low and represented direct time involved in developing the impact study. The total fully loaded cost for the program was $32,984.

Table 27. Cost Summary for 48 Participants in Three Courses

Item	Cost
Facilitation fees, three courses @$3,750	$11,250
Program materials, 48 @ $35 per participant	1,680
Meals and refreshments, three days @ $28 per participant	4,032
Facilities, nine days @ $120	1,080
Participants' salaries plus benefits (35% factor)	12,442
Coordination and evaluation	2,500
Total Costs	**$32,984**

ROI Calculation

Two ROI calculations are possible with use of the total monetary benefits and total cost of the program. The first is the BCR, which is the ratio of the monetary benefits divided by the costs:

$$\text{BCR} = \frac{\$71,760}{\$32,984} = 2.18\%$$

In essence, this suggests that, for every dollar invested, 2.18 dollars are returned. When using the actual ROI formula, this value becomes:

$$\text{ROI (\%)} = \frac{\$71,760 - \$32,984}{\$32,984} \times 100 = 118\%$$

This ROI calculation is interpreted as follows: For every dollar invested, a dollar is returned, and another $1.18 is generated. The ROI formula is consistent with ROI for other types of investment. It is, essentially, earnings divided by investment. In this case, the ROI exceeds the 50 percent target.

Intangibles

This program generated significant intangible benefits:

- Increased job satisfaction

- Improved teamwork

- Increased confidence

- Improved customer service

- Improved image with customers

- Greater involvement

Communication of Results

It was important to communicate the results of this evaluation to the senior executives who requested a program, to the sales associates who were part of it, and to other personnel who were affected by it. First, the senior executives needed the information to make a decision. In a face-to-face meeting, lasting approximately one hour, the training and development staff distributed an executive summary and the results. Results included all six types of data with the recommendation that the program be implemented throughout the store chain.

The participants received a two-page summary of the data, showing the results of the questionnaire and the business impact and ROI achieved from the process. There was some debate about whether to include the ROI in the summary. Eventually it was added in an attempt to share more information with the participants.

The participants' managers in the electronics department received the executive summary of the information and participated in a conference call with the training and development staff. This group needed to see the benefits of training, since they had to alter and rearrange schedules to cover the jobs while the participants were in training.

Finally, the training staff received a detailed impact study (approximately 100 pages), which was used as a learning document to help them understand more about this type of evaluation. This document became the historical record about the data collection instruments and ROI analysis.

As a result of the communication of the impact study, senior executives decided to implement the program throughout the store chain. For all six types of data, the results were very positive with a very high ROI, significantly exceeding the target. The implementation proceeded with the senior executives' request that the sales data for the three target stores be captured for the remainder of the year to see the actual one-year impact of the program. While the issue of taking one year of data based on a three-month snapshot appears to be conservative, since the second- and third-year data are not used, this provided some assurance that the data do indeed hold up for the year. At the end of the year, the data actually exceeded the three-month performance snapshot.

Insights and Considerations

This evaluation provides some important insights into the ROI Methodology. In the past, the store chain evaluated pilot programs primarily on Level 1 data (reactions from both the participants and their managers) coupled with the sales presentation from the vendor. The ROI approach provides much more data to indicate the success of training. In essence, companies can use Level 4 and 5 data for making a funding decision instead of deciding based solely on Level 1.

From a statistical significance viewpoint, the small sample size does not allow for making an inference about the other stores at a 95 percent confidence interval. In essence, it is impossible to say that the other stores would have the same results as the three in question. However, the economics of the evaluation and the practicality of the pilot implementation drove the sample size in this and most other cases. While it is important to note that a statistical inference cannot be made, it is equally important to remember two points:

- The six types of data represent much more data than previously used to evaluate these types of programs.

- Most managers do not make other funding decisions based on data that has been collected, analyzed, and reported at a 95 percent confidence level.

In this case, the company wanted to test a program to determine the feasibility of rolling it out. Based on the 118% ROI from the results from three stores, the data were significant enough for decision makers to move forward with the program.

Another observation about this. application of the ROI Methodology is that it represents a simple case allowing for a control group arrangement. Many other situations are not this simple and often require other techniques to isolate the effects of the program.

Also, this case study focuses on increasing sales—a simple measure to collect and convert using profit margin. Other measures, such as measures of productivity, quality, and time savings, are also relatively simple, because standard values often exist. However, when standard values do not exist, other data conversion techniques must be pursued. When a measure cannot be converted to money using the available techniques or within the cost constraints under which the program is being evaluated, the improvement in the measure is reported as an intangible benefit.

CHAPTER 6: ROI FORECASTING

The Bottomline on ROI is intended to provide a brief introduction to the ROI Methodology. While ROI forecasting goes beyond that brief introduction, the interest in the topic is greater than ever before. This chapter presents the bottomline on ROI forecasting.

ROI at Multiple Levels

ROI can be developed at different times and with different levels of data. Ease, convenience, and costs involved in capturing ROI create trade-offs in accuracy and credibility. As shown in Table 28, there are five distinct time intervals during program implementation when the ROI can be developed. The relationship between the timing of the ROI and the factors of credibility, accuracy, cost, and difficulty is also shown in the table.

Table 28. ROI at Different Levels

ROI With:	Data Collection Timing – (Relative to the Initiative)	Credibility	Accuracy	Cost to Develop	Difficulty
		Least Credible	Least Accurate	Least Expensive	Least Difficult
Pre-Program Forecast	Before				
Level 1 Data	During				
Level 2 Data	During				
Level 3 Data	After				
Level 4 Data	After				
		Most Credible	Most Accurate	Most Expensive	Most Difficult

Pre-Program Forecasts

Pre-program forecasts are ideal when deciding between two or more programs designed to solve the same problem. They also serve well when considering one very expensive program or deciding between one or more delivery channels. Whatever the need for pre-program forecasting, the process is similar to post-program ROI, only simpler and less expensive.

Figure 8 shows the basic forecast model. As shown, an estimate of the change in results data that is expected to be influenced by the program is the first step in the process. From there, data conversion, cost estimates, and the calculation are the same as in post-program analysis. The anticipated intangibles in forecasting are speculative, but they can be indicators of which measures may be influenced beyond those included in the ROI calculation. The difference between the pre-program model and the standard post-program model is that the step of isolating the effects of the program is omitted. It is assumed that the estimated results refer to the influence on the program under evaluation.

Figure 8. ROI Pre-Program Model

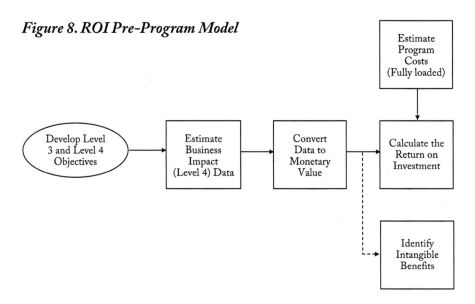

Table 29 presents ten steps in developing a pre-program ROI forecast.

Table 29. Ten Steps to an ROI Forecast

1. Develop Level 3 and 4 objectives with as many specifics as possible.
2. Estimate or forecast the monthly improvement in the business impact data (ΔP).
3. Convert the business results data to monetary values (V).
4. Develop the estimated annual impact (ΔI) in monetary terms by multiplying the monthly improvement times the value times 12:
$\Delta I = \Delta P \times V \times 12$.
5. Factor additional years into the analysis if a program will have a significant useful life beyond the first year.
6. Estimate the fully loaded cost of the program (C).
7. Calculate the forecasted ROI using the total projected benefits and the estimated cost in the standard ROI formula:

$$ROI\ (\%) = \frac{\Delta I - C}{C} \times 100$$

8. Use sensitivity analysis to develop several potential ROI values with different levels of potential improvements.
9. Identify potential intangible benefits by obtaining input from those most knowledgeable of the situation.
10. Communicate the ROI projection and anticipated intangibles with care and caution.

Table 30 shows the output of a pre-program forecast for the interactive selling skills program described in Chapter 5. Multiple sources of data were asked to estimate the monthly change in performance in sales that could occur by investing in the program. Sales were converted to profit using the 2% profit margin. They were then annualized and compared to the estimated fully loaded cost of the program. The last column in the table is the forecast ROI for each source. From there, each forecast is ranked in terms of credibility, and a decision is made based on the best estimate.

Table 30. Sample Output of Pre-Program Forecast

Measure: Sales

Profit Margin: 2%

Source	Monthly Improvement	Value (2%)	Annual Impact	Program Cost	ROI
SME	$25,000	$500	$6,000	$5,000	20%
Vendor	$50,000	$1,000	$12,000	$5,000	140%
Participant	$30,000	$600	$7,200	$5,000	44%
Supervisor	$28,000	$560	$6,720	$5,000	34%

When targeting multiple measures, it is good practice to use sensitivity analysis to consider all combinations of results. Table 31 demonstrates this process where there are two measures of concern: sales and customer complaints. As shown in the table, there are different forecast ROIs as sales increase and complaints decrease. While it might be argued that these data are not helpful, given the difference in the forecasts, others would say that they do provide some insight into the potential success of a program. The key is to remember that a forecast is different than an ROI objective. Forecasts are indicators of what could happen; objectives are indicators of what should happen.

Table 31. Sample Output of Sensitivity Analysis

Potential Sales Increase	Potential Complaint Reduction	Potential ROI
$25,000	10	60%
$25,000	20	90%
$25,000	30	120%
$30,000	10	90%
$30,000	20	120%
$30,000	30	150%
$50,000	10	120%
$50,000	20	150%
$50,000	30	180%

Pilot Program

A more accurate forecast of program success is through a small-scale pilot, developing an ROI based on post-program data. There are five steps to this approach:

1. As in the pre-program forecast, develop Level 3 and 4 objectives.

2. Initiate the program on a small scale without all the bells and whistles. This keeps the cost low without sacrificing the fundamentals of the program.

3. Fully implement the program with one or more of the typical groups of individuals who can benefit from the program.

4. Develop the ROI using the ROI Methodology for post-program analysis.

5. Decide whether to implement the program throughout the organization based on the results of the pilot program.

Using a pilot post-program evaluation as the ROI forecast allows stakeholders to make decisions based on actual results versus anticipated results.

Level 1 ROI

A simple approach to forecasting ROI for a new program is to add a few questions to the standard Level 1 evaluation questionnaire. As in the case of a pre-program forecast, the data are not as credible as in an actual post-program evaluation; however, a Level 1 evaluation does rely on data from participants who have actually attended the program.

Table 32 presents a series of questions that can develop a forecast ROI at the end of a program. Using this series of questions, participants detail how they plan to use what they have learned and the results that they expect to achieve. They are asked to convert their anticipated accomplishments into an annual monetary value and show the basis for developing the values; they adjust their values with a confidence estimate, which makes the data more credible while allowing participants to reflect on their uncertainty with the process. The monetary benefits of the program are calculated and then compared to the projected program costs to calculate the ROI. While not as reliable as actual data, this process provides some indication of potential program success.

Table 32. Questions for Level 1 ROI

- As a result of this program, what specific actions will you attempt as you apply what you have learned?

  _____

  _____

  _____

- Indicate what specific measures, outcomes, or projects will change as a result of your action.

  _____

  _____

  _____

- As a result of these anticipated changes, estimate (in monetary values) the benefits to your organization over a period of one year. $_____

  What is the basis of this estimate?

  _____

  _____

  _____

- What confidence, expressed as a percentage, can you put in your estimate? (0% = no confidence; 100% = certainty) _____%

Level 2 ROI

Other approaches to forecasting include the use of Level 2 test data. A reliable test, reflecting the content of a learning program, is validated against job performance data (impact measures). With a statistically significant relationship between test scores and job performance, test scores should relate to improved job performance. The performance can be converted to monetary value, and the test scores can then be used to estimate the monetary impact from the program. When compared to projected costs, the ROI is forecasted.

This technique has slightly more credibility than a Level 1 forecast, because it relies on test data and statistical analysis. Unfortunately, many programs do not use validated tests as measures of learning, so this technique is not as feasible as some people would like.

Level 3 ROI

A final approach to forecasting ROI is with Level 3 data. This approach attracts the attention of many practitioners who simply cannot access business impact data. The original approach is based on utility analysis and has been modified so that its use is more widespread. While still a subjective approach, it can be useful in forecasting value added by improving competencies. This simple approach to forecasting ROI using improvement with competencies is to:

1. Identify the competencies being developed in the program.
2. Determine the percentage of jobs requiring these skills.
3. Determine the monetary value of the competencies using salary and benefits of participants.
4. Determine the increase in skill level due to the program.
5. Calculate the monetary benefits of the improvement.
6. Compare the monetary benefits to the cost of the program.

Table 33 presents a basic example of forecasting ROI using Level 3 data.

Table 33. Forecasting ROI at Level 3

Ten supervisors attend a four-day developmental program that costs $65,000 fully loaded. The average salary (plus benefits factor) of the 10 supervisors is $110,000. Following the six steps below, the program team forecasted the ROI based on improvement in participants' supervisory skills.

1. Identify competencies: Supervisory skills, including:
   Role and responsibilities
   Communication skills
   Planning, controlling, and evaluating work
   Motivation
   Managing diversity

2. Determine percentage of job requiring these skills: 85% (average of group)

3. Determine the monetary value of the competencies using salary and benefits of participants: $93,500 per participant

   Multiply percentage of skills used on the job by the value of the job.

   $$\$110,000 \times 85\% = \$93,500$$

   Total dollar value of the competencies for the group: $93,500 × 10 = $935,000.

4. Determine increase in skill level due to program: 15% increase (average of group based on comparison of pre- versus post-program, on-the-job competency assessment)

5. Calculate the monetary benefits of the improvement: $140,250

   Multiply the dollar value of the competencies by the improvement in skill level.

   $$\$935,000 \times 15\% = \$140,250$$

   Compare the monetary benefits to the cost of the program: ROI of 116%

   $$ROI = \frac{\$140,250 - \$65,000}{\$65,000} \times 100 = 116\%$$

Level 4 ROI

Finally, the ROI can be developed from Level 4 business impact data by converting measures to monetary values and comparing those values to program costs. This is not a forecast; rather, it is the type of post-program evaluation that has been described throughout this book. Calculating ROI using post-program Level 4 business impact data is the preferred approach, but examining ROI calculations at other times and with other levels is sometimes necessary.

A Word of Caution

Forecasting is an excellent tool when an actual ROI study is not feasible. A word of caution, however; if you do forecast, do so frequently. The process needs to be pursued regularly to build experience and a history of use. Also, it is always helpful to conduct an actual ROI study following a forecast and compare the results to develop better skills for the forecasting process. Be sure to secure input from those who know the program and the measures best, and expect the forecast, from whomever you receive it, to include bias. Lastly, remember there is a difference between an ROI forecast and an ROI objective; forecasts indicate what could happen, objectives indicate what should happen.

CHAPTER 7: ROI IMPLEMENTATION

To this point, the book has described the fundamental elements of the ROI Methodology. Chapter 5 described a simple case study demonstrating the application of the ROI Methodology. Chapter 6 described the basics of forecasting ROI at multiple levels. But how does an organization really make ROI work? This chapter addresses the barriers—both realistic and perceived—that can get in the way of successful implementation. It presents a process for selecting technology to support the measurement and evaluation practice and ends by offering a few steps to get started.

Barriers to Implementation

The first step toward successful implementation of any process is to understand the potential barriers. Implementation of the ROI Methodology is no different. Founded or unfounded, these barriers are real and need to be addressed.

Costs and Time

A comprehensive measurement and evaluation process that includes ROI will add costs and time to a program's implementation, although the added amounts will likely not be excessive. The additional costs should be no more than 3–5 percent of the departmental budget. The additional investment in ROI should be offset by the results achieved from implementation (e.g., the elimination or prevention of unproductive or unprofitable programs). The cost/time barrier alone stops many ROI implementation plans early in the process. However, there are a few shortcuts and cost-saving approaches shown in Table 34 that can help to reduce the cost of the actual implementation.

Table 34. Shortcuts to ROI Implementation

TIPS AND TECHNIQUES TO REDUCE THE COST OF IMPLEMENTING THE ROI PROCESS

- Build evaluation into the performance improvement process.
- Develop criteria for selecting program measurement levels.
- Plan early for evaluation.
- Share responsibilities for evaluation.
- Require participants to conduct major steps.
- Use shortcut methods for major steps.
- Use estimates.
- Develop internal capability.
- Streamline the reporting process.
- Utilize technology.

Source: Patti P. Phillips and Holly Burkett. *Managing Evaluation Shortcuts.* Infoline. Alexandria, VA: ASTD Press, 2001.

Lack of Skills

Many staff members either do not understand ROI or do not have the skills necessary to apply the process within the scope of their responsibilities. The typical program evaluation also focuses more on qualitative feedback data than quantitative results. Consequently, a tremendous barrier to implementation is the discrepancy in the overall orientation, attitude, and skills of staff members engaged in program design, development, implementation, and evaluation. Some suggestions for building skills in ROI include the following:

- Attending public workshops
- Becoming certified in ROI implementation

- Conducting internal workshops

- Starting with less comprehensive evaluations and building toward more advanced projects

- Participating in evaluation and ROI networking forums

Faulty or Inadequate Initial Analysis

All too often, inadequate analysis leads teams to the wrong conclusions, thereby bringing them to the wrong solutions. Management requests to chase a popular fad or trend in the industry are often based on faulty analysis of the problem or opportunity. If a program is not necessary or not based on business needs, it may not produce enough benefits to overcome the costs. An ROI calculation for an unnecessary program will likely yield a negative value. To avoid offering an unnecessary or inappropriate program (which can lead to less than desired results), develop or enhance the performance consulting process. Become engaged with the client in order to gain a deeper understanding of their needs. This will help to ensure that the appropriate program or solution is implemented, yielding a greater ROI.

Fear

Some staff members do not pursue ROI because of fear of failure or fear of the unknown. Fear of failure appears in several ways. Some staff members will be concerned about the consequences of a negative ROI. They perceive the evaluation process as an individual performance evaluation rather than a process-improvement tool. For others, a comprehensive measurement process can stir up the common fear of change and all the unknowns that change brings. Although it is often based on unrealistic assumptions and a lack of knowledge of the process, fear is so strong that it becomes a real barrier to many ROI implementations. Making sure that staff members understand the process and its intent is key to dissolving these fears.

Discipline and Planning

Successful implementation of the ROI Methodology requires significant planning and a disciplined approach to keep the process on track. It requires implementation schedules, transition plans, evaluation targets, ROI analysis plans, measurement and evaluation policies, and follow-up schedules. The practitioner may not have enough discipline and determination to stay the course, and this inevitably becomes a barrier, particularly if there is no immediate pressure to measure ROI. If clients or other executives are not demanding ROI evaluation, the staff may not allocate the time necessary for planning and coordination. Also, other pressures and priorities often eat into the time necessary for ROI implementation. Planning the work and working the plan are key to successful implementation.

False Assumptions

Many professionals have false assumptions about ROI that deter them from pursuing implementation. Some typical false assumptions are:

- ROI can only be applied to a few narrowly focused programs.

- Senior managers do not want to see the results of programs expressed in monetary values.

- If clients do not ask for ROI, it should not be pursued.

- If the CEO does not ask for ROI, then he or she does not expect it.

While these assumptions are usually based on incorrect data or misunderstandings, they still form realistic barriers that impede the progress of ROI implementation. Again, understanding the methodology and the need for ROI are critical factors in overcoming this barrier.

Technology Selection

Technologies to collect, analyze, and report data are available to support the implementation of the ROI Methodology. Some are designed specifically to support this particular model, while others are flexible enough to apply regardless of the type of evaluation approach used. As organizations build capacity in measurement, evaluation, and ROI, technologies will become even more important.

A common fallacy in using technologies and various software applications is the ability to do the work. While technology eases the pain of collecting, analyzing, and reporting data, it does not do the work required to ensure practitioners take the appropriate measures, analyze data correctly, and report results in a way that resonates with the audience. Many readers of this book are clear on the purpose that technology serves in measurement and evaluation, but there are others who rely on the companies developing the technology to provide appropriate guidance on data collection design and data analysis techniques. Understanding the fundamentals of every step in the measurement and evaluation process is important. Although this does not mean everyone has to be an expert, a learning and development professional must have enough grounding that they can ask critical questions that will ensure they collect the right data the right way, analyze data to address those questions appropriately, and report the output in such a way that the information is useful to decision makers.

Dr. Kirk Smith, former Assistant Professor at Western Carolina University and Director of ROI Implementation at ROI Institute (and to whom this book is dedicated) suggested that deciding on the appropriate technology to support measurement and evaluation is much like any decision that arises when making a major investment in the organization (Smith, 2010). The first step is to establish criteria for selection.

Establish Criteria

The top three questions to answer in order to establish criteria for selecting a tool are:

1. What do you want to know from your data?

2. How are you going to use the data?

3. Who are the intended users of the information?

Once the answers to the question are clear, the next step is to identify and prioritize the intended uses of the information. The answers and actions will form the basis for developing the criteria to make the decision about the right technology. Examples of criteria include:

- Keep costs to a minimum

- Make reporting easy

- Allow for customization

- Provide access to raw data

- Automate report distribution

- Make implementation easy

Establishing the criteria for the technology prior to discussing the options is important. Decision analysis is not about identifying choices and making a case for one specific alternative. Instead, it is about establishing what needs to be accomplished and then finding the alternative that best achieves that outcome (Kepner and Tregoe, 1997).

Discern the Musts from the Wants

When the criteria are defined, the next step is to classify them in terms of what "Must" be available from the technology and what you would "Want" from the technology. A criterion can be a Must if the answer is "yes" to the following three questions:

1. Is it mandatory (required)?

2. Is it measurable (a limit can be set)?

3. Is it realistic (can be met)?

For example, the objective "keep costs to a minimum" cannot be a Must, because it is not measurable with a limit. The word "minimum" is too vague to be a measurable limit. Any time an objective contains the words "minimize," "maximize," or "optimize," it cannot be a Must. The only Must in the above criteria is "access to raw data." This requirement is measurable with a limit, in that the raw data can be downloaded or not, and it is realistic, in that the technology that allows access to raw data does exist.

A set of criteria might have one to three Musts; all other criteria represent Wants. Musts indicate which criteria are a priority; Wants are the deciding factor.

Weigh the Wants

The next step is to weigh the Wants. Give the most important Wants a weight of 10. Other Wants are weighted relative to the 10s. For example, if another Want is half as important as a 10, then weigh it as a 5.

Generate Alternatives

Next, generate alternatives by identifying possible choices, and screen the alternatives against the Must. If an alternative cannot satisfy the Must, then it is eliminated as a choice.

Evaluate Alternatives

The next step is to evaluate the Wants relative to the performance of each alternative. Score the best-performing alternative for each Want with a 10. As before, score the other alternatives relative to the best performer. For example, if Alternative 1 performs a 10 out of 10 in terms of keeping costs to a minimum, Alternative 2 is slightly more expensive, and Alternative 4 is even more expensive, then Alternative 10 would be given a score of 10 for performance, Alternative 2 might be given a score of 7, and Alternative 4 might be given a score of 4. These scores are then multiplied by the weight of importance that the criterion has in the decision making. So, in the case of the criterion "keeping costs to a minimum," Alternative 1 would have a total score of 70 (7 x 10); Alternative 2 would have a total score of 49 (7 x 7); and Alternative 3 would have a total score of 28 (7 x 4). Table 35 summarizes the scores for each criterion and the total scores for each alternative. As shown in Table 35, Alternative 1 has the highest score and would therefore be the top candidate for selection.

Table 35. Evaluating Alternatives

Criteria	Weight	Alternatives			
		1	2	3	4
Keep costs to a minimum	7	10/70	7/49		4/28
Make reporting easy	6	5/30	10/60		8/48
Allow for customization	10	10/100	10/100		10/100
Provide access to raw data	M	GO	GO	NO GO	GO
Automate report distribution	4	3/12	8/32		10/40
Easy implementation	6	10/60	7/42		3/18
Totals		272	193		234

Adapted from "Selecting Technology to Support Evaluation," Kirk Smith. In *ASTD Handbook of Training Evaluation*. Patti P. Phillips, Alexandria, VA: ASTD Press, 2010, p. 304.

Identify Risks

As a final step in the process, it is important to identify any risks associated with the highest-scoring alternative. If selecting the highest-scoring technology poses a significant risk, go to the next-highest-scoring alternative and do the same risk analysis. Some questions to ask during the risk assessment are:

- What could go wrong short- and long-term if we implement this solution?

- What are the implications of being close to a Must limit?

- What disadvantages are associated with this alternative?

- Did I make any invalid assumptions about this alternative?

Working through the described process can help select the right technologies to support measurement and evaluation, particularly when it comes to the more expensive technology solutions.

Next Steps

Now that the ROI Methodology has been explained, a simple case study described, and suggestions have been offered for consideration when preparing for the implementation of the process, the question is: "What now?" How does someone get started evaluating programs using the ROI Methodology? Table 36 provides a checklist of steps to help newcomers to the ROI Methodology begin the implementation process. As progress is made and issues surface, there are numerous resources available to assist in implementing ROI. Some of those resources are listed in the reference section at the back of this book.

Table 36. Next Steps

IMPLEMENTING ROI

- Assess progress and readiness for ROI implementation.
- Organize a task force or network to initiate the process.
- Develop and publish a philosophy or mission statement concerning accountability and ROI for all programs.
- Clarify roles and responsibilities of project team members.
- Develop a transition plan detailing the steps necessary to implement ROI successfully.
- Set targets for evaluating programs at the various levels of evaluation.
- Develop guidelines to ensure that ROI is implemented completely and consistently.
- Build staff skills.
- Establish a management support system or champions of ROI.
- Enhance management support of and commitment to participation in the implementation of ROI.
- Achieve short-term results by evaluating one program at a time.
- Communicate results to selected audiences.
- Teach the process to others to enhance their understanding of ROI.
- Establish a quality review process to ensure that the evaluation process remains consistent and credible.

The Bottomline

So what is the bottomline on ROI? For generations, ROI has been used to show the value of programs, projects, and processes within organizations. The ROI calculation is the financial ratio used by accountants, CFOs, and executives to measure the return on all types of investments. The term ROI is already familiar to executives and operational managers. It is not a new, fly-by-night catchphrase with an unknown meaning that can only be explained through elaborate presentations and will only be understood in a very small area of an organization.

The ROI Methodology described in this book represents the use of the classic ROI economic indicator, yet it goes beyond a cost-benefit comparison. It provides a balanced viewpoint of the impact of all types of programs, processes, and projects by taking into consideration participant reaction, learning, application of new skills and knowledge, and business impact achieved through the programs. The process presents the complete picture of program success. Furthermore, by including the critical step of isolating the effects of the program, the impact on business can be further linked to specific programs. The process presented in this book is based on sound research and conservative standards. Although not all programs should be evaluated at the ROI level, for those meeting specific criteria, ROI is a credible approach to providing evidence of a program's financial impact on an organization. A thorough and complete understanding of ROI can help to eliminate fears and overcome barriers to its implementation.

CHAPTER 8: FREQUENTLY ASKED QUESTIONS

Today's leaders must show accountability for the investments made in their programs and processes. Many leaders have found that actually measuring the ROI of a few select high-profile programs is an excellent way to show fiscal responsibility for key projects and initiatives. For almost two decades, we at the ROI Institute have been assisting organizations with this important issue. These questions come from conferences and workshop participants as well as clients with whom we work on consulting assignments. This chapter presents answers to the 25 most frequently asked questions about ROI.

1. **How does the ROI used in the context of program evaluation differ from the ROI used by financial staff?**
    The classic definition of ROI is "earnings divided by the investment." In the context of calculating the ROI for programs such as learning and development, performance improvement, HR, quality, and marketing, the earnings become the net benefits from the program (monetary benefits minus the costs), and the investment is the actual program cost. The challenge lies in developing the actual monetary benefits in a credible way.

2. **Do I have to learn finance and accounting principles to understand the ROI Methodology?**
    No—many of the principles of finance and accounting don't relate to what is needed to develop the ROI in programs such as those described in this book. However, it is important to understand issues such as revenue, profit, and cost. Ultimately,

the payoff of programs and projects will be based on either direct cost savings or additional profit generated. It is helpful to understand the nature and types of costs and the different types of profits and profit margins in order to make sense of the results.

3. **Do I have to know statistics to understand ROI?**
Only very basic statistical processes are necessary to develop most ROI impact studies. It is rare for anything to be needed beyond simple descriptive statistics. Sometimes hypothesis testing and correlations are necessary. These are simple concepts and are, by design, simplified as much as possible in the processes described in the book.

4. **Is ROI just one single number? How can you communicate a program's value with a number?**
The ROI Methodology develops six types of data, with the actual ROI calculation being only one of them. The six types of data are:

Reaction and Planned Action

Learning

Application and Implementation

Business Impact

ROI

Intangibles

5. **Aren't the levels of evaluation out-of-date and not applicable?**
Although the concept of levels has been around for some time, it remains valid and applicable, and the ROI Methodology adds a new and critical dimension to the original approach. The original four steps developed by Don Kirkpatrick show how the data must be developed to generate value from a program. The

data are arranged in a chain of impact that must exist if the learning, performance improvement, and HR initiatives are to have business impact, which ultimately becomes business value. The chain of impact can be broken at any point; this means that correlations do not always exist between the levels, because there are barriers to success at any level. Although a few researchers take issue with the four levels, this is still the most widely used foundation for evaluation. ROI becomes the fifth level and is the consequence of the program expressed in monetary terms. These levels of results are applicable in all types of decision-making situations. A topic, content, or issue is presented, the audience reacts, acquires more information, applies (or does not apply) the information, and, as a consequence, some impact occurs. ROI (Level 5) brings in a new set of data—money—both in the numerator and the denominator. Because of the logic behind this chain of impact and the need for different types of data, the concept of levels is alive and well and being implemented far beyond the learning, performance improvement, and HR industries.

6. **Isn't ROI based only on subjective estimates?**
   Estimates are used only when other methods are not readily available or become too time-consuming or expensive to obtain. When estimates are made, they are adjusted for the error of the estimate to improve their credibility. In essence, the results of estimates are understated. Estimates, when necessary, are usually used in four instances:
   1. When records are not readily available to show the improvement or, in a forecast situation, where the data are unknown.
   2. When isolating the effects of a program.
   3. When converting data to monetary values.
   4. When calculating the costs (a widely accepted finance practice).

In every case, there are many alternatives to estimates, and these alternatives are often recommended. Estimates are used routinely in some situations because they become the preferred method and are accepted by stakeholders or they may be the only way to obtain the needed data.

7. **Isn't ROI too complicated for most non-technical professionals?**

The ROI calculation itself is very simple: net benefits divided by costs. The processes needed to arrive at the benefits follow a methodical step-by-step sequence, with guiding principles used along the way. The costs are developed using guidelines and principles as well. What complicates the process are the many options available at each step. However, these options are critical because of the various situations, programs, and projects that need to be evaluated and the different environments and settings in which they occur. Having standards to consider when selecting between options reduces the complication.

8. **Doesn't evaluation leading up to ROI cost too much?**

The cost for a study all the way through to ROI may represent as much as 5–10 percent of the budget for the entire program or project, although this percentage varies considerably depending on the scope. It is also important to note that, in most organizations, every program is evaluated at some level. The total cost of all evaluation, including selected ROI studies, is usually in the range of 3–5 percent of the total departmental budget.

9. **Is it possible to isolate the effects of my program from other factors?**

This is the most difficult and challenging issue, but it is always possible, even if estimates are used. Some of the most sophisticated and credible processes involve control groups, trend line analysis, and forecasting models. Other times, less-sophisticated techniques are used, such as expert estimation and customer input. When estimates are used, the data should be adjusted for the error of the estimate. Always strive to carve out the data directly related to the program or project.

10. **Is it true that the ROI process does not reveal program weaknesses or strengths?**
    The ROI Methodology captures six types of data. At Levels 1, 2, and 3, data always capture deficiencies or weaknesses in the process. At Level 3, the process requires collecting data about the barriers to success and the enablers that increase success.

11. **Is it true that the ROI process does not result in recommendations for improvement?**
    Each impact study using the ROI Methodology contains a section for recommendations for improvement. It is essential that this tool be utilized, first and foremost, as a process-improvement tool. Recommendations for change are always appropriate, even when studies reflect a very successful project.

12. **Is it appropriate to conduct an ROI study for every program?**
    Only a few select programs should be subjected to evaluation all the way through to the fifth level of evaluation (ROI). Ideal targets include programs that are very expensive, strategic, operationally focused, and highly visible, and those that involve large target audiences and have management attention in terms of their accountability. In most organizations using this methodology, only about 5–10 percent of the programs are selected for ROI analysis each year.

13. **Which programs are <u>not</u> suited for ROI analysis (but may still achieve a positive ROI)?**
    Certain programs should not be evaluated all the way through to ROI. The following programs are not appropriate for ROI:

mandatory programs, compliance programs, legally required initiatives, specific operational job-related programs, brief programs, information-sharing programs, entry-level programs, new-to-the-job programs, and programs intended to align the individual with the organization.

14. **Who is using the ROI Methodology?**
Virtually all types of organizations in the United States and around the world are using the ROI Methodology. To date, almost 5,000 private sector, public sector, and social sector organizations have formally implemented ROI through skill-building and ROI Certification. In essence, thousands of organizations are utilizing the ROI Methodology through an informal implementation in various parts of their organization. In addition, almost 25,000 specialists and managers have taken either a one- or two-day ROI workshop, and more than 12,000 individuals have participated in five-day comprehensive certification workshops.

15. **What types of applications are typical for ROI analysis?**
The applications can vary, but usually include sales training, supervisory training, team building, executive development, competency systems, software utilization, leadership development, diversity, orientation systems, compensation and benefits, reward systems, skill-based pay, career management, major projects, meetings and events, communication strategies, and wellness initiatives. These topics make excellent targets for the ROI Methodology, as has been documented with case studies in the literature.

16. **How can I learn more about ROI?**
There are many options available to learn about ROI. Several books, case studies, and templates have been published, with many of them published or made available through ROI

Institute (www.roiinstitute.net). Additional resources are available through www.amazon.com. In partnership with HRDQ, the publisher of this book, we are offering a kit that includes this book, a Participant Workbook, and a Facilitator Guide to assist organizations in developing fundamental skills. For those individuals who want to become proficient in the process, the ROI Institute offers a five-day certification workshop about 20 times a year. Additionally, on-site consulting and coaching is an option. For more information on these opportunities, visit www.roiinstitute.net.

17. Can ROI be used on the front end of a project as a forecasting tool?

ROI forecasting is an important part of the ROI Methodology. This process uses credible data and expert input and involves estimating the improvement (projected benefits) that will occur if a program is implemented. Projected benefits are compared to projected costs to develop the forecasted ROI.

18. How does ROI compare to a Balanced Scorecard?

The ROI process generates six types of data (reaction, learning, application, business impact, ROI, and intangibles), which comprise a scorecard. The Balanced Scorecard process developed by Kaplan and Norton (1996) suggests four categories of data (learning and growth, internal business processes, finance, and customer). The data generated with the ROI Methodology can all be grouped into one of these four categories if desired. In addition, the ROI process adds two other capabilities not normally contained in the Balanced Scorecard methodology: it provides a technique to isolate the effects of a program, and it shows the costs versus benefits of a particular program or initiative. Thus, the ROI Methodology will complement the Balanced Scorecard process.

19. **How can I secure support for ROI in my organization?**
Building support for the ROI Methodology is an important issue. Top executives will usually support the process when they realize the types of data that will be generated. Most of the resistance comes from those directly involved in programs, because they do not understand ROI and how it is to be used in the organization. Involving them in implementing the process and properly using data to drive improvements helps to lower the resistance. Efforts to implement any major change program will apply to the implementation of the ROI Methodology.

20. **How can I minimize staff resistance to the ROI Methodology?**
Most staff will have some resistance to the ROI Methodology, unless they see the value it can bring to their work. Involvement, education, and process improvement are key issues. It is often the fear of ROI that generates resistance—a fear based on misunderstandings about the process and how the data will be used. The ROI Methodology should be implemented as a process-improvement tool and not as a performance evaluation tool for the staff. No one wants to develop a tool that will reflect unfavorably on them in their performance review. Improvement in key decisions about the use of ROI will help to minimize resistance. Resistance will also be minimized when steps are taken to ensure that the data are communicated properly, improvements are generated, and the data are not abused or misused.

21. **Should I conduct an ROI study on my own program?**
If possible, the person evaluating the program should be independent of the program. It is important for the stakeholders to understand that the person conducting the study is objective and removed from certain parts of the study, such as the data collection and the initial analysis. Sometimes these issues can

be addressed in a partnering role or in limited outsourcing opportunities—whether for data collection or analysis. In other situations, the issue must be addressed, and the audience must understand that steps have been taken to ensure that the data were collected and analyzed objectively and reported completely.

22. Are there any standards for ROI?

The ROI Methodology, as developed by Jack and Patti Phillips and their associates, contains standards referred to as "Guiding Principles." (See page 98.) These provide consistency for the analysis, with a conservative approach. The conservative approach builds credibility with the stakeholders.

23. What type of background is necessary for learning the ROI Methodology?

It is helpful for the individual to understand the business in which the studies will be developed and to have knowledge about operations, products, and financial information. In addition, the individual should not have a fear of numbers. Although the ROI Methodology does not involve much statistical analysis, it does involve some data analysis. Excellent communication skills are needed to develop the various documents describing results and to present those results to a variety of stakeholder groups. Finally, the ability to partner with many individuals is extremely important. This requires much focus, contact, and collaboration with the client—this is a very client-focused methodology. The individual must be willing to meet with the key sponsors of programs and to build the relationships necessary to capture the data and communicate the data to them.

24. How is ROI on technology-enabled projects developed?

Applying the ROI Methodology to technology-enabled projects is the same as any other process, program, or solution. The monetary value of the benefits from the project is compared to the cost of the project. Many individuals assume that the benefits of a project remain the same and that only the costs to implement the project change due to the technology. In reality, the benefits may change as well. An ROI study should be conducted to show the actual benefits of implementing the project, not just the cost savings achieved by changing approaches. For example, when an organization opts to implement technology-enabled learning versus in-person classroom training, the reason for doing so is often to reduce the cost of delivery. That cost savings shows up in the denominator of the equation, not in the numerator (the benefits side of the equation). The benefits derived from a technology-enabled training program are based on what people do with what they learn from the content of the program. The change to delivering learning via technology versus the classroom is a change in the delivery—but the content and the learning transfer strategy are the keys to gaining benefit and, ultimately, a positive ROI. As a result, if the content design and delivery and the learning transfer strategy are weaker through the technology-enabled training than through the classroom training, a lower ROI is likely.

25. How do you calculate the ROI on the ROI?

This is a very good question to raise in terms of the payoff of using this methodology. The important issue is the value of implementing the process itself. While literally hundreds of organizations are reporting the benefits and successes, it is helpful to understand the internal payoff in the organization. The improvements and changes resulting from an impact study are tallied from one study to another and compared to the actual cost of the implementation. This, in essence, can generate the return on investment for utilizing this process. This approach is recommended for most major implementations.

REFERENCES

Alliger, G. M., and S. I. Tannenbaum. 1997. A meta-analysis of the relations among training criteria. *Personnel Psychology* 50, no. 2: 341–358.

Anthony, R. N., and J. S. Reece. 1983. *Accounting text and cases.* New York, NY: McGraw-Hill.

American Productivity and Quality Center. 2000. *The corporate university: Measuring the impact of learning.* Houston: American Productivity and Quality Center.

ASTD. 2016. *State of the industry report.* Alexandria, VA: ATD.

Broad, M. L., and J. W. Nestrom. 1992. *Transfer of training.* Boston, MA: Perseus Books.

Chief Learning Officer Business Intelligence Board 2016 Measurement and Metrics. info.clomedia.com/2016-measurement-metrics

Friedlob, F. J., and G. T. Plewa. 1996. *Understanding return on investment.* San Francisco, CA: John Wiley & Sons, Inc.

Horngren, C. T. 1982. *Cost accounting.* Englewood Cliffs, NJ: Prentice Hall.

i4cp and ROI Institute. 2016. The Promising State of Human Capital Analytics. www.roiinstitute.net/promising-state-human-capital-analytics/

Kearsley, G. 1982. *Costs, benefits, and productivity in training systems.* Reading, MA: Addison-Wesley Publishing.

Kepner, C.H., and B.B. Tregoe. 1997. *The new rational manager.* Princeton, NJ: Princeton Research Press.

Kirkpatrick, D. L. 1994. *Evaluating training programs: The four levels.* San Francisco, CA: Berrett-Koehler Publishers.

Mosley, J., and S. Larson. 1994. A qualitative application of Kirkpatrick's model for evaluation workshops and conferences. *Performance & Instruction* 33, no. 8: 3-5.

Nas, T. F. 1996. *Cost-benefit analysis.* Thousand Oaks, CA: Sage Publications.

Phillips, J. J. 1983. *Handbook of training evaluation and measurement methods.* Houston, TX: Gulf Publishing.

Phillips, J. J. 1995. Corporate training: Does it pay off? *William & Mary Business Review.* Summer: 6–10.

Phillips, J. J. 1996a. Was it the training? *Training and Development* (March).

Phillips, J. J. 1996b. How much is the training worth? *Training and Development* (April): 20–24.

Phillips, J. J. 1997a. *Return on investment in training and performance improvement programs.* Waltham, MA: Elsevier Butterworth-Heinemann.

Phillips, J. J. 1997b. *Handbook of training evaluation and measurement methods.* 3rd ed. Waltham, MA: Elsevier Butterworth-Heinemann.

Phillips, J. J., and P. P. Phillips. 2007. *Show me the money.* San Francisco, CA: Berrett-Koehler.

Phillips, J. J., and P. P. Phillips. 2010. *Measuring for success: What CEOs really think about learning investments.* Alexandria, VA: ASTD.

Phillips, P. P., and J. J. Phillips. 2007. *The value of learning: how organizations capture value and ROI.* San Francisco, CA: Pfeiffer.

Phillips, P. P. 2010. Calculating the return on investment. *ASTD handbook of measuring and evaluating training.* Alexandria, VA: ASTD.

Phillips, P.P., and H. Burkett. 2001. *Managing evaluation shortcuts.* Infoline. Alexandria, VA: ASTD.

Sibbett, D. 1997. Harvard Business Review: 75 years of management ideas and practice 1922–1977. *Harvard Business Review.* Sep/Oct 1997 Supplement, 75:5.

Smith, K. 2010. Selecting Technology to Support Evaluation. In Phillips, P. P. *ASTD handbook of training evaluation.* Alexandria, VA: ASTD.

Thompson, M. S. 1980. *Benefit-cost analysis for program evaluation.* Thousand Oaks, CA: Sage Publications.

Warr, P., C. Allan, and K. Birdi. 1999. Predicting three levels of training outcome. *Journal of Occupational and Organizational Psychology.* 72: 351–375.

ABOUT THE AUTHOR

Patti P. Phillips, Ph.D.

Dr. Patti P. Phillips is president and CEO of ROI Institute, the leading source of ROI competency building, implementation support, networking, and research. A renowned expert in measurement and evaluation, she helps organizations implement the ROI Methodology in 70 countries around the world. She serves as chair of the Institute for Corporate Productivity People Analytics Board, Principal Research Fellow for The Conference Board, board chair of the Center for Talent Reporting, and ATD CPLP Certification Institute Fellow. Patti also serves on the faculty of the UN System Staff College in Turin, Italy; Escuela Bancaria y Comercial in Mexico City, Mexico; and The University of Southern Mississippi's Ph.D. in Human Capital Development program. Her work has been featured on CNBC, *EuroNews,* and in over a dozen business journals.

Before co-founding the ROI Institute, Patti served as a researcher and manager of market research for a large electric utility. Patti's academic accomplishments include a Ph.D. in International Development and a master's degree in public and private management. She is certified in ROI evaluation and has been awarded the designations of Certified Professional in Learning and Performance and Certified Performance Technologist.

Patti contributes to a variety of journals and has authored or edited over 75 books on the subjects of measurement, evaluation, analytics, and ROI. Recent titles include: *The Business Case for Learning* (HRDQ and ATD Press, 2017); *Chief Talent Officer* 2nd ed. (Routledge, 2016); *Handbook of Training Evaluation and Measurement Methods,* 4th ed. (Routledge, 2016); *Accountability in Human Resource Management,* 2nd ed. (Routledge, 2016); *Measuring the Success of Employee Engagement* (ATD Press, 2016); *Making Human Capital Analytics Work* (McGraw-Hill, 2015); *Real World Training Evaluation* (ATD Press, 2015);

Measuring the Success of Leadership Development (ATD Press, 2015); *High-Impact Human Capital Strategy* (AMACOM, 2015); *Maximizing the Value of Consulting* (Wiley, 2015); *Performance Consulting* 3rd ed. (Berrett-Koehler, 2015); *Measuring ROI in Environment, Health, and Safety* (Wiley-Scrivener, 2014); *Measuring ROI in Employee Relations and Compliance* (SHRM, 2014); *Measuring the Success of Learning Through Technology* (ASTD Press, 2014); *Measuring the Success of Organization Development* (ASTD Press, 2013); *Survey Basics* (ASTD, 2013); *Measuring the Success of Sales Training* (ASTD Press, 2013); *Measuring ROI in Healthcare* (McGraw-Hill, 2012); *10 Steps to Successful Business Alignment* (ASTD Press, 2012); *Measuring the Success of Coaching* (ASTD Press, 2012); *The Bottomline on ROI* 2nd Edition (HRDQ, 2012); and *Measuring Leadership Development: Quantify Your Program's Impact and ROI on Organizational Performance* (McGraw-Hill, 2012). Patti Phillips can be reached at **patti@roiinstitute.net**.

ABOUT THE DEVELOPER OF THE ROI METHODOLOGY

Jack J. Phillips, Ph.D.

Dr. Jack J. Phillips is chairman of ROI Institute. Phillips is a world-renowned expert on accountability, measurement, and evaluation. Phillips provides consulting services for Fortune 500 companies and major global organizations. The author or editor of more than 100 books, he conducts workshops and presents at conferences throughout the world.

Phillips has received several awards for his books and work. On three occasions, *Meeting News* named him one of the 25 Most Powerful People in the Meetings and Events Industry, based on his work on ROI. The Society for Human Resource Management presented him an award for one of his books and honored a Phillips ROI study with its highest award for creativity. The Association for Talent Development (formerly, The American Society for Training and Development) gave him its highest award, Distinguished Contribution to Workplace Learning and Development, for his work on ROI. His work has been featured in the *Wall Street Journal, BusinessWeek,* and *Fortune* magazine. He has been interviewed by several television programs, including CNN.

His expertise in measurement and evaluation is based on more than 27 years of corporate experience in the aerospace, textile, metals, construction materials, and banking industries. Dr. Phillips has served as training and development manager at two Fortune 500 firms, as senior human resource officer at two firms, as president of a regional bank, and as management professor at a major state university.

Dr. Phillips regularly consults with clients in manufacturing, service, and government organizations in 70 countries in North and South America, Europe, Africa, Australia, and Asia.

Jack and his wife Patti have authored or edited over 125 books. Their most recent publications include: *The Business Case for Learning* (HRDQ and ATD Press, 2017); *Chief Talent Officer,* 2nd ed. (Routledge,

2016); *Handbook of Training Evaluation and Measurement Methods*, 4th ed. (Routledge, 2016); *Measuring the Success of Employee Engagement* (ATD Press, 2016); *Accountability in Human Resource Management*, 2nd ed. (Routledge, 2016); *Real World Evaluation Training* (ATD Press, 2016); *High-Impact Human Capital Strategy* (AMACOM, 2015); *Maximizing the Value of Consulting* (Wiley, 2015); *Performance Consulting*, 3rd ed. (Berrett-Koehler, 2015); *Measuring the Success of Leadership Development* (ATD Press, 2015); *Making Human Capital Analytics Work* (McGraw-Hill, 2015); *Measuring ROI in Environment, Health, and Safety* (Wiley, 2014); *Measuring the Success of Learning Through Technology* (ASTD Press, 2014); *Measuring the Success of Organization Development* (ASTD Press, 2013); *Survey Basics* (ASTD Press, 2013); *Measuring the Success of Sales Training* (ASTD Press, 2013); *Measuring ROI in Healthcare* (McGraw-Hill, 2012); *Measuring the Success of Coaching* (ASTD Press, 2012); *Measuring Leadership Development: Quantify Your Program's Impact and ROI on Organizational Performance* (McGraw-Hill, 2012); *10 Steps to Successful Business Alignment* (ASTD Press, 2012); *The Green Scorecard: Measuring the Return on Investment in Sustainability Initiatives* (Nicholas Brealey, 2011); and *Project Management ROI* (Wiley, 2011). Patti and Jack have also served as authors and series editors for the Measurement and Evaluation Series published by Pfeiffer (2008), which includes a six-book series on the ROI Methodology and a companion book of 14 best-practice case studies.

Dr. Phillips has undergraduate degrees in electrical engineering, physics, and mathematics; a master's degree in decision sciences from Georgia State University; and a Ph.D. in Human Resource Management from the University of Alabama. He has served on the boards of several private businesses—including two NASDAQ companies—and several nonprofits and associations, including the American Society for Training and Development, the International Society for Performance Improvement, and the National Management Association. Jack Phillips can be reached at **jack@roiinstitute.net**.

PUT YOUR MONEY WHERE YOUR MOUTH IS

The Bottomline on ROI

For decades, senior leaders simply accepted learning and development as a necessary "people" cost. However, today is different. Today, senior leaders are asking the questions that make some trainers cringe. They want to know what value training and development initiatives bring to the organization. They want to know the business impact, and they want to know the ROI.

New from subject matter experts Jack Phillips and Patti Phillips, the Bottomline on ROI workshop complements this book and illustrates and reinforces the learning with real-world examples and exercises. Whether you are new to the ROI Methodology or are looking for ways to generate support for ROI within your organization, together these tools will provide you with a fundamental understanding of ROI and how it can be implemented.

Learning Outcomes:

- Identify the benefits of developing ROI

- Learn how to assess an organization's readiness for ROI

- Understand the concept and assumptions of ROI

- Discover the criteria for effective ROI implementation

- Learn the ROI Methodology, a model that will produce a balanced set of measures

- Learn a communication process model for effective communication during the ROI process

- Discover how to get started implementing the ROI Methodology

The comprehensive Facilitator Guide includes easy-to-follow instructions for delivering a half-day, full-day, or two-day learning experience. The Participant Workbook comes complete with exercises, activities, quizzes, tools, and templates.

ABOUT ROI INSTITUTE®

ROI Institute, Inc. is the leading resource on research, training, and networking for practitioners of the ROI Methodology. Founders and owners Jack J. Phillips, Ph.D. and Patti P. Phillips, Ph.D. are the leading experts in the application of ROI to learning, HR, and performance improvement programs.

Founded in 1993, ROI Institute is a service-driven organization assisting professionals in improving their programs and processes through the use of the ROI Methodology. This methodology is a critical tool for measuring and evaluating programs with over 22 different applications in more than 70 countries.

ROI Institute offers a variety of consulting services, learning opportunities, and publications. In addition, it conducts research activities for organizations internally, as well as for other enterprises, public sector entities, industries, and interest groups, globally.

ROI Certification

ROI Institute is the only organization offering ROI Certification to build expertise in implementing ROI evaluation and sustaining the measurement and evaluation process in your organization. When competencies in the ROI Methodology have been demonstrated, certification is awarded. There is no other process that provides access to the same level of expertise as our ROI Certification. To date, over 12,000 individuals have participated in this process.

For more information on certification, workshops, consulting and research, please visit us on the web at: www.roiinstitute.net, email info@roiinstitute.net, or call us at 205.678.8101.

Build Capability in the ROI Methodology

ROI Institute offers a variety of workshops to help you build capability in the ROI Methodology. Among the many workshops offered through the ROI Institute are:

One-day Bottomline on ROI Workshop—provides the perfect introduction to all levels of measurement, including the most sophisticated level, ROI. Learn the key principles of the Phillips ROI Methodology and determine whether your organization is ready to implement the process.

Two-day ROI Competency Building Workshop—the standard ROI workshop on measurement and evaluation, this two-day program involves discussion of the ROI Methodology process, including data collection, isolation methods, data conversion, and more.

ABOUT HRDQ

Since its inception in 1977, HRDQ has been in the business of creating off-the-shelf resources for developing great people skills. We offer a range of experiential games, assessments, simulations, and ready-to-use programs in practical, easy-to-use formats suitable for trainers and classroom facilitators of any experience level. Our products cover a range of interpersonal skills, including collaboration, leadership, communication, emotional intelligence, coaching, team building, influencing, creativity and innovation, negotiation, and managing conflict.